MISSISSIPPI TRAVEL GUIDE 2024

Exploring Mississippi: Discovering History, Culture, and Natural Beauty.

BY

TILDA ROMERO

Copyright © 2024 TILDA ROMERO.

All Rights Reserved.

Table of Contents

Disclaimer 5

Introduction 7

    Introduction to the Magnolia State 9

    Quick Facts and Travel Tips 15

    Best Times to Visit 20

Chapter 1: Jackson: Heart of Mississippi 25

    History and Heritage: Exploring Jackson's Past 25

    Top Attractions: Museums, Parks, and More 28

    Food and Drink: A Culinary Journey 35

    Nightlife and Entertainment: Where to Go After Dark 39

Chapter 2: The Mississippi Delta: Birthplace of the Blues ... 43

    Discovering the Delta's Music Heritage 43

    Must-Visit Historical Sites 45

    Outdoor Adventures: From Hiking to River Tours 48

    Delta Cuisine: Unique Flavors to Savor 50

Chapter 3: Coastal Mississippi: Sun, Sand, and Seafood 55

    Beaches and Boardwalks: Top Spots for Sun Seekers 55

    Seafood Delights: A Guide to Coastal Dining 58

Casinos and Nightlife: Entertainment by the Gulf 60

Nature and Wildlife: Exploring Coastal Preserves 63

Chapter 4: Oxford and the University Scene 67

Literary Landmarks: Walking in Faulkner's Footsteps 67

College Town Vibes: Exploring Ole Miss 70

Best Eats: From Cafes to Fine Dining 74

Cultural Highlights: Museums, Art, and Music 78

Chapter 5: Vicksburg: History on the River 83

Civil War Sites: Reliving the Past 83

Riverfront Attractions: What to See and Do 86

Local Cuisine: Southern Comfort Foods 89

Shopping and Souvenirs: Where to Find Unique Gifts 94

Chapter 6: Natchez: Southern Charm and Antebellum Splendor 99

Antebellum Homes: A Step Back in Time 99

Riverboat Cruises: Exploring the Mighty Mississippi 101

Festivals and Events: Year-Round Celebrations 104

Dining and Nightlife: Best Spots to Eat and Drink 108

Chapter 7: The Natchez Trace Parkway: Scenic Drives and Hidden Gems 111

Top Scenic Stops: Must-See Points of Interest 111

Outdoor Activities: Hiking, Biking, and More 114

Historical Landmarks: Tracing the Past 116

Chapter 8: Small Town Treasures 119

Discovering Mississippi's Quaintest Towns.....................119

Unique Festivals and Local Events 122

Regional Cuisines: From BBQ to Biscuits 126

Chapter 9: Practical Information 129

Getting There and Around 129

Accommodation Guide: Best Places to Stay 132

Travel Resources and Useful Contacts 135

Conclusion 139

Disclaimer

Dear Reader,

Thank you for choosing the Mississippi Travel Guide 2024. We are thrilled to be your companion on this exploration of the Magnolia State. However, we must inform you that this guide does not include images. Here's why:

Focus on Information: Our primary goal is to provide you with comprehensive and detailed information about Mississippi's attractions, history, accommodations, and practical travel tips. By focusing solely on text, we ensure that the content remains concise, informative, and easy to navigate.

Personalized Experience: We believe in sparking your imagination and allowing you to envision the beauty of Mississippi through descriptive writing. This approach encourages a more personalized travel experience, where you can create mental images based on our vivid descriptions and recommendations.

Practicality and Convenience: Omitting images also enhances the practicality of this guide. It allows for a lightweight and portable format, making it easy for you to carry and reference during your travels without the bulk of a photo-heavy book.

Accessibility: We aim to make this guide accessible to all readers, including those who prefer or require text-only formats due to technological limitations or personal preferences.

While we understand the allure of visual content, we believe that the absence of images in this guide does not diminish its value. Instead, it encourages you to immerse yourself in the words, stories, and practical advice provided, enhancing your anticipation and curiosity about the wonders awaiting you in Mississippi.

We sincerely hope that this guide enriches your journey and helps you discover the best of what Mississippi has to offer. Happy travels!

Introduction

Welcome to the Mississippi Travel Guide 2024, your ultimate companion to exploring the rich heritage, vibrant culture, and diverse landscapes of the Magnolia State. Mississippi, a land where history and modernity intertwine, offers an abundance of experiences for every traveler. From the soulful rhythms of the Delta blues to the sun-drenched beaches of the Gulf Coast, this guide will navigate you through the best that Mississippi has to offer.

In this book, you'll uncover the stories of Jackson, the heart of Mississippi, where history and heritage come alive in its museums, parks, and lively neighborhoods. Discover the roots of American music in the Mississippi Delta, the birthplace of the blues, and immerse yourself in the region's unique cultural and culinary traditions.

Head south to Coastal Mississippi, where sun, sand, and seafood await. Explore pristine beaches, savor fresh Gulf seafood, and enjoy the bustling nightlife of the coastal towns. Journey to Oxford, a literary haven and home to the University of Mississippi, where Southern charm and intellectual pursuits blend seamlessly.

Experience Vicksburg's historical significance with its Civil War sites and riverfront attractions, and marvel at the antebellum splendor of Natchez, where grand homes and riverboat cruises transport you back in time. Drive along the scenic Natchez Trace Parkway, stopping at hidden gems and historical landmarks along the way.

Beyond the well-known destinations, this guide will lead you to Mississippi's small-town treasures, where you'll find unique festivals, local events, and regional cuisines that reflect the state's rich cultural tapestry.

Packed with practical information, including travel tips, accommodation options, and useful contacts, the Mississippi Travel Guide 2024 is designed to provide you with everything you need for a memorable adventure. Whether you're a history buff, a foodie, an outdoor enthusiast, or simply seeking a new destination to explore, Mississippi welcomes you with open arms and endless possibilities. Let's embark on this journey together and uncover the magic of Mississippi.

Introduction to the Magnolia State

The Essence of Mississippi

Mississippi, named after the mighty river that forms its western border, is a state steeped in history and tradition. From the rolling hills of the north to the fertile plains of the Delta, and the sun-kissed beaches of the Gulf Coast, Mississippi's diverse geography offers something for everyone. The state's nickname, the Magnolia State, reflects its abundance of magnolia trees, whose fragrant blossoms are a symbol of southern hospitality.

History and Heritage

Mississippi's history is a rich tapestry woven with stories of Native American tribes, European explorers, and African American communities. The state played a pivotal role in the Civil War and the Civil Rights Movement, leaving behind a legacy that is both complex and deeply significant.

Notable Historical Sites:

Vicksburg National Military Park

Address: 3201 Clay St, Vicksburg, MS 39183

A crucial site in the Civil War, this park preserves the history of the Siege of Vicksburg and offers insightful tours and exhibits.

Mississippi Civil Rights Museum

Address: 222 North St #2205, Jackson, MS 39201

This museum provides a powerful and moving account of the struggle for civil rights in Mississippi and the broader United States.

Culture and Arts

Mississippi is a cultural melting pot, with influences from African American, Native American, and European traditions. The state is renowned for its contributions to music, particularly the blues, which was born in the Mississippi Delta.

Must-Visit Cultural Sites:

B.B. King Museum and Delta Interpretive Center

Address: 400 2nd St, Indianola, MS 38751

This museum honors the life and legacy of blues legend B.B. King and explores the history of the blues.

The Mississippi Museum of Art

Address: 380 S Lamar St, Jackson, MS 39201

Showcasing a diverse collection of American art, this museum is a cultural cornerstone of the state capital.

Natural Beauty

Mississippi's natural beauty is both diverse and breathtaking. From the dense forests and rolling hills of the north to the expansive wetlands and sandy beaches of the south, nature lovers will find plenty to explore.

Top Natural Attractions:

Tishomingo State Park

Address: 105 Co Rd 90, Tishomingo, MS 38873

Known for its stunning rock formations and scenic hiking trails, this park is a haven for outdoor enthusiasts.

Gulf Islands National Seashore

Address: 3500 Park Rd, Ocean Springs, MS 39564

Offering pristine beaches, nature trails, and abundant wildlife, this seashore is perfect for a day of relaxation and exploration.

Culinary Delights

Mississippi's culinary scene is a feast for the senses, with a rich array of flavors that reflect the state's diverse cultural heritage. From soul food to seafood, there's something to satisfy every palate.

Must-Try Dishes:

Catfish

Widely available across the state, try it at The Old Country Store (Address: 18801 US-61, Lorman, MS 39096), where it's served buffet-style with all the fixings.

Tamales

The Delta is famous for its unique take on tamales. Don't miss Doe's Eat Place (Address: 502 Nelson St, Greenville, MS 38701), a legendary spot for this local delicacy.

Festivals and Events

Mississippi hosts a variety of festivals and events throughout the year that celebrate its rich cultural heritage and community spirit. From music festivals to historical reenactments, there's always something happening.

Notable Festivals:

Juke Joint Festival

Location: Clarksdale, MS

This festival celebrates the Delta blues with live music, food, and cultural events in the heart of Clarksdale.

Natchez Spring Pilgrimage

Location: Natchez, MS

A tradition since 1932, this event offers tours of historic homes and gardens, showcasing the city's antebellum architecture and history.

Practical Information

When planning your visit to Mississippi, it's important to have some practical information at hand to ensure a smooth and enjoyable trip.

Travel Tips:

Best Times to Visit: Spring (March to May) and Fall (September to November) offer mild weather and numerous festivals.

Getting Around: Renting a car is recommended for exploring the state, as public transportation options are limited in rural areas.

Useful Contacts:

Mississippi Tourism Office:

Address: 501 N West St, Jackson, MS 39201

Phone: (601) 359-3297

Website: visitmississippi.org

Quick Facts and Travel Tips

Quick Facts

State Nickname: The Magnolia State

Capital: Jackson

Population: Approximately 2.95 million

Area: 48,430 square miles

Time Zone: Central Standard Time (CST)

Official Language: English

State Bird: Northern Mockingbird

State Flower: Magnolia

State Tree: Magnolia

Major Rivers: Mississippi River, Yazoo River, Pearl River

Major Industries: Agriculture, Manufacturing, Tourism, Gaming

Travel Tips

Best Time to Visit

Mississippi enjoys a humid subtropical climate, making it a year-round destination. However, the best times to visit are spring (March to May) and fall (September to November)

when the weather is mild and comfortable. Summers can be hot and humid, especially in the southern parts of the state, while winters are generally mild, with occasional cold spells.

Getting Around

By Car: The most convenient way to explore Mississippi is by car. Major highways such as I-55, I-20, and I-10 provide easy access to various parts of the state. Renting a car is recommended if you plan to explore multiple cities and regions.

Public Transportation: Public transit options are limited, but cities like Jackson and Biloxi offer bus services. For longer distances, consider Greyhound or Megabus services.

Air Travel: Jackson-Medgar Wiley Evers International Airport (JAN) is the main airport, with other regional airports in Gulfport (GPT) and Tupelo (TUP). Direct flights to major hubs make air travel a viable option.

Train Travel: Amtrak's City of New Orleans route runs from Chicago to New Orleans, with stops in Jackson and other Mississippi towns, offering a scenic and relaxing way to travel.

Accommodation

Mississippi offers a range of accommodations, from budget motels to luxury resorts. For a unique experience, consider staying in a bed-and-breakfast or an antebellum home. Notable options include:

Monmouth Historic Inn & Gardens: 1358 John A Quitman Blvd, Natchez, MS 39120. A charming antebellum mansion offering elegant rooms and beautiful gardens.

The Alluvian Hotel: 318 Howard St, Greenwood, MS 38930. A luxurious boutique hotel known for its Southern hospitality and comfort.

Beau Rivage Resort & Casino: 875 Beach Blvd, Biloxi, MS 39530. A premier destination on the Gulf Coast with a casino, spa, and fine dining.

Dining and Cuisine

Mississippi's culinary scene is a delightful mix of Southern comfort food, seafood, and barbecue. Don't miss trying these local specialties:

Catfish: A staple in Mississippi, often fried and served with hushpuppies and coleslaw. Try it at Cock of the Walk (141 Madison Landing Cir, Ridgeland, MS 39157).

Barbecue: Slow-cooked, smoky meats are a must. The Pig & Pint (3139 N State St, Jackson, MS 39216) is a local favorite.

Tamales: Unique to the Delta, these tamales are different from their Mexican counterparts. Sample them at Doe's Eat Place (502 Nelson St, Greenville, MS 38701).

Seafood: The Gulf Coast is renowned for fresh seafood. Mary Mahoney's Old French House (110 Rue Magnolia, Biloxi, MS 39530) offers an unforgettable dining experience.

Cultural Etiquette

Mississippi is known for its Southern hospitality. Here are a few tips to ensure a respectful and pleasant visit:

Greetings: Politeness is highly valued. Address people with "sir" or "ma'am," and a warm smile and handshake go a long way.

Dress Code: Casual attire is generally acceptable, but dressing neatly is appreciated, especially when visiting historical sites or dining in upscale restaurants.

Tipping: Standard tipping practices apply. Leave 15-20% in restaurants, a few dollars for hotel housekeeping, and tip cab drivers and valet attendants accordingly.

Safety Tips

Weather: Be aware of the weather, especially during hurricane season (June to November) along the Gulf Coast. Keep an eye on local forecasts and heed any warnings.

Wildlife: Mississippi's natural areas are home to various wildlife. When hiking or exploring outdoors, stay on designated trails and be cautious of snakes and insects.

Personal Safety: Like any travel destination, stay aware of your surroundings, particularly in unfamiliar areas. Keep valuables secure and avoid walking alone at night in less-populated areas.

Emergency Contacts

Emergency Services: Dial 911 for police, fire, or medical emergencies.

Visitor Information: Mississippi Tourism Office - (601) 359-3297

Jackson-Medgar Wiley Evers International Airport: (601) 939-5631

Best Times to Visit

Spring (March to May)

Spring is arguably the best time to visit Mississippi. The weather is mild, with temperatures ranging from the mid-60s to mid-80s Fahrenheit, making it perfect for outdoor activities and sightseeing. The state's gardens and parks are in full bloom, creating picturesque landscapes.

Key Events and Festivals:

Natchez Spring Pilgrimage (March to April): This is a must-see event where historic homes and gardens in Natchez are open to the public. Visitors can tour antebellum mansions and enjoy traditional Southern hospitality. Address: 640 S Canal St, Natchez, MS 39120.

Jackson's Mal's St. Paddy's Parade (March): A vibrant parade celebrating St. Patrick's Day with music, food, and festivities. Address: Downtown Jackson, MS.

Summer (June to August)

Summer in Mississippi is hot and humid, with temperatures often exceeding 90°F. Despite the heat, this is a great time to enjoy the state's numerous water activities and coastal attractions.

Key Events and Festivals:

Biloxi's Fourth of July Fireworks (July 4): A spectacular display over the Gulf of Mexico. Address: Biloxi Beach, Biloxi, MS.

Neshoba County Fair (late July): Known as "Mississippi's Giant House Party," this week-long fair includes horse racing, concerts, and political speeches. Address: 16800 MS-21, Philadelphia, MS 39350.

Tips:

Stay hydrated and wear light, breathable clothing.

Visit coastal areas like Gulfport and Biloxi to enjoy the beaches and ocean breezes.

Fall (September to November)

Fall is another fantastic time to visit Mississippi. The weather cools down, making it ideal for exploring the outdoors and attending numerous festivals. The fall foliage, particularly in the northern parts of the state, adds a beautiful backdrop to your travels.

Key Events and Festivals:

Mississippi Delta Blues & Heritage Festival (September): Held in Greenville, this festival celebrates the rich blues heritage of the Delta. Address: 1335 Hwy 82 W, Greenville, MS 38701.

Cruisin' The Coast (early October): A week-long event featuring classic cars cruising along the Mississippi Gulf Coast. Address: Various locations along the Gulf Coast, starting from Bay St. Louis to Biloxi.

Tips:

Pack layers, as temperatures can vary, especially in the evenings.

Enjoy outdoor activities like hiking and biking in areas such as the Natchez Trace Parkway.

Winter (December to February)

Winter in Mississippi is relatively mild, with temperatures ranging from the mid-40s to mid-60s Fahrenheit. This is a great time to explore indoor attractions, historical sites, and cultural events without the crowds.

Key Events and Festivals:

Christmas in Natchez (December): Natchez comes alive with holiday lights, tours of decorated historic homes, and festive events. Address: Various locations in Natchez, MS.

Mardi Gras Celebrations (February): Coastal cities like Biloxi and Gulfport host lively Mardi Gras parades and parties. Address: Downtown Biloxi and Gulfport, MS.

Tips:

This is the off-peak season, so you can often find better deals on accommodations and attractions.

Don't miss the Vicksburg National Military Park, where you can tour the battlefield and learn about Civil War history without the summer heat. Address: 3201 Clay St, Vicksburg, MS 39183.

Year-Round Attractions

Regardless of when you visit, some attractions in Mississippi offer enjoyment throughout the year:

Mississippi Civil Rights Museum: Learn about the civil rights movement in Mississippi. Address: 222 North St #2205, Jackson, MS 39201.

Elvis Presley Birthplace: Visit the birthplace of the King of Rock 'n' Roll in Tupelo. Address: 306 Elvis Presley Dr, Tupelo, MS 38804.

Mississippi Museum of Art: Explore a wide range of art exhibits in Jackson. Address: 380 S Lamar St, Jackson, MS 39201.

Chapter 1: Jackson: Heart of Mississippi

History and Heritage: Exploring Jackson's Past

Old Capitol Museum

100 S State St, Jackson, MS 39201

Begin your journey at the Old Capitol Museum, housed in the original state capitol building constructed in 1839. This National Historic Landmark showcases the history of Mississippi from its statehood in 1817 through the Civil War. The museum's exhibits include artifacts, photographs, and interactive displays that chronicle the political, social, and economic development of the state. The grand architecture and beautifully restored interiors provide a glimpse into the grandeur of 19th-century government buildings.

Mississippi Civil Rights Museum

222 North St, Jackson, MS 39201

Next, visit the Mississippi Civil Rights Museum, an essential stop for anyone interested in understanding the struggle for racial equality in America. This powerful museum is divided into eight galleries, each detailing different aspects of the Civil Rights Movement. From the brutality of Jim Crow laws to the bravery of Freedom Riders, the museum's exhibits use film, audio recordings, and personal stories to bring the history to life. A highlight is the interactive gallery where visitors can listen to firsthand accounts from those who lived through this tumultuous period.

Medgar Evers Home Museum

2332 Margaret W Alexander Dr, Jackson, MS 39213

A visit to Jackson's historical sites wouldn't be complete without stopping at the Medgar Evers Home Museum. Medgar Evers, a prominent civil rights activist and NAACP field secretary, lived in this modest house with his family until his assassination in 1963. The home has been preserved as a museum, offering a poignant look into Evers' life and the impact of his work. Guided tours provide detailed insights into his contributions to the Civil Rights Movement and the personal sacrifices he made in the fight for justice.

Eudora Welty House and Garden

1119 Pinehurst St, Jackson, MS 39202

For a literary perspective on Jackson's history, visit the Eudora Welty House and Garden. Eudora Welty, a Pulitzer

Prize-winning author, lived and wrote in this home for over seventy-six years. The house has been meticulously restored to reflect its appearance during Welty's lifetime, complete with her personal library, original furnishings, and family photographs. The garden, designed by Welty's mother, offers a serene escape and a glimpse into the author's private world.

Mississippi State Capitol

400 High St, Jackson, MS 39201

No exploration of Jackson's heritage is complete without a tour of the Mississippi State Capitol. Completed in 1903, this Beaux-Arts building serves as the seat of Mississippi's government. Free guided tours are available, providing visitors with insights into the building's history, architecture, and the legislative process. The interior is adorned with stunning stained glass, marble floors, and intricate woodwork, highlighting the craftsmanship of the period.

Smith Robertson Museum and Cultural Center

528 Bloom St, Jackson, MS 39202

The Smith Robertson Museum and Cultural Center, located in Jackson's first public school for African American children, celebrates the cultural heritage of African

Americans in Mississippi. Exhibits cover a wide range of topics, from slavery and Reconstruction to the modern Civil Rights Movement. The museum also features works by African American artists and highlights contributions made by African Americans to the state's history and culture.

Farish Street Historical District

Farish St, Jackson, MS 39202

Take a stroll through the Farish Street Historical District, once the bustling center of African American life in Jackson. This district was home to thriving businesses, entertainment venues, and social organizations from the early 20th century through the 1960s. While some buildings have been lost to time, efforts are ongoing to preserve and revitalize this historically significant area. Walking tours are available, providing context and stories about the people and places that made Farish Street a cultural hub.

Top Attractions: Museums, Parks, and More

Jackson: A Hub of History and Culture

Mississippi Civil Rights Museum

Address: 222 North Street, Jackson, MS 39201

Opened in 2017, the Mississippi Civil Rights Museum chronicles the struggle for civil rights in Mississippi. Through its eight galleries, visitors are taken on a journey from the early days of slavery to the civil rights movement of the 1960s. The museum's powerful exhibits, including interactive displays and poignant artifacts, offer an in-depth look at the bravery and resilience of those who fought for equality.

Mississippi Museum of Art

Address: 380 South Lamar Street, Jackson, MS 39201

Home to an impressive collection of American art, the Mississippi Museum of Art features works from the 19th century to the present. Highlights include pieces by notable Southern artists and a beautiful outdoor Art Garden. The museum frequently hosts special exhibitions, art classes, and community events, making it a vibrant cultural center in Jackson.

LeFleur's Bluff State Park

Address: 3315 Lakeland Terrace, Jackson, MS 39216

This 305-acre park, located along the Pearl River, offers a natural escape within the city. Visitors can enjoy a variety of outdoor activities, including hiking, fishing, and picnicking.

The park also features the Mississippi Museum of Natural Science, where exhibits on the state's diverse ecosystems and wildlife are displayed.

The Mississippi Delta: Birthplace of the Blues

B.B. King Museum and Delta Interpretive Center

Address: 400 2nd Street, Indianola, MS 38751

Dedicated to the life and legacy of blues legend B.B. King, this museum in Indianola provides a comprehensive look at the history of the blues and its impact on American music. The museum includes memorabilia, recordings, and interactive exhibits that celebrate King's contributions and the broader cultural significance of the blues.

Delta Blues Museum

Address: 1 Blues Alley, Clarksdale, MS 38614

Located in the historic freight depot in Clarksdale, the Delta Blues Museum is the oldest music museum in Mississippi. It showcases the history and heritage of the Delta blues through a collection of artifacts, photographs, and musical instruments. The museum also hosts live performances and educational programs, making it a must-visit for music enthusiasts.

Coastal Mississippi: Sun, Sand, and History

Lynn Meadows Discovery Center

Address: 246 Dolan Avenue, Gulfport, MS 39507

This award-winning children's museum in Gulfport offers interactive exhibits and educational programs designed to inspire and engage young minds. From the outdoor play areas to the art studio and science exhibits, the Lynn Meadows Discovery Center provides a fun and enriching experience for families.

Beauvoir: The Jefferson Davis Home and Presidential Library

Address: 2244 Beach Boulevard, Biloxi, MS 39531

Beauvoir, the post-war home of Confederate President Jefferson Davis, offers a glimpse into the history of the Civil War and Southern life in the 19th century. The estate includes the main house, gardens, a Confederate cemetery, and a museum with exhibits on Davis's life and legacy.

Oxford: A Literary and Academic Gem

Rowan Oak

Address: 916 Old Taylor Road, Oxford, MS 38655

The former home of famed author William Faulkner, Rowan Oak is now a museum dedicated to his life and works. Visitors can tour the Greek Revival house and its grounds, gaining insight into Faulkner's writing process and the inspiration he drew from the Southern landscape.

University of Mississippi Museum

Address: University Avenue and 5th Street, Oxford, MS 38677

Located on the campus of Ole Miss, this museum houses an extensive collection of Southern folk art, Greek and Roman antiquities, and 19th-century scientific instruments. The museum also features rotating exhibitions and educational programs that highlight the region's cultural and artistic heritage.

Vicksburg: A City Steeped in History

Vicksburg National Military Park

Address: 3201 Clay Street, Vicksburg, MS 39183

This expansive park preserves the site of the Civil War's pivotal Battle of Vicksburg. Visitors can explore the battlefield, tour the historic Vicksburg National Cemetery, and view the USS Cairo, a Union ironclad gunboat. The park's visitor center offers detailed exhibits and films that provide context to the battle and its significance.

Old Courthouse Museum

Address: 1008 Cherry Street, Vicksburg, MS 39183

Housed in a National Historic Landmark building, the Old Courthouse Museum contains an impressive collection of artifacts related to the history of Vicksburg and the Civil War. Exhibits include Confederate flags, antique furniture, and items from daily life in the 19th century.

Natchez: Antebellum Elegance and Riverfront Charm

Longwood

Address: 140 Lower Woodville Road, Natchez, MS 39120

Known for its unique octagonal design, Longwood is the largest octagonal house in the United States. This antebellum mansion offers guided tours that explore its unfinished interior and the fascinating story of its construction during the Civil War.

Natchez National Historical Park

Address: 640 South Canal Street, Natchez, MS 39120

This park encompasses several historic sites, including Melrose, a beautifully preserved antebellum estate, and the

William Johnson House, which tells the story of a free African American barber and diarist. The park provides a comprehensive look at the region's history and architecture.

Exploring the Great Outdoors

Tishomingo State Park

Address: 105 County Road 90, Tishomingo, MS 38873

Nestled in the foothills of the Appalachian Mountains, Tishomingo State Park is known for its stunning scenery and diverse recreational opportunities. Visitors can hike the park's trails, fish in Bear Creek, and explore unique rock formations and historic sites.

DeSoto National Forest

Address: 654 West Frontage Road, Wiggins, MS 39577

Covering over 500,000 acres, DeSoto National Forest offers a vast expanse of wilderness for outdoor enthusiasts. Activities include hiking, camping, horseback riding, and birdwatching. The forest's diverse ecosystems, from pine savannas to wetland areas, provide a habitat for a wide range of wildlife.

Food and Drink: A Culinary Journey

Jackson: A Hub of Culinary Diversity

Start your culinary adventure in Jackson, the state capital, where you'll find a melting pot of flavors. For a taste of classic Southern cuisine, head to Walker's Drive-In (3016 N State St, Jackson, MS 39216). This upscale diner offers dishes like seared scallops and duck confit, showcasing local ingredients with a gourmet twist.

Another must-visit is The Manship Wood Fired Kitchen (1200 N State St #100, Jackson, MS 39202), where the Mediterranean meets Southern cuisine. Their wood-fired pizzas and roasted meats are a testament to the innovative culinary scene in Jackson.

For a more casual yet equally delightful experience, visit Bulldog Burger Company (6111 Ridgewood Rd Suite G, Jackson, MS 39211). Known for their gourmet burgers and craft beers, it's a perfect spot for a laid-back meal.

Delta Delights: Clarksdale and Beyond

The Mississippi Delta, often referred to as the birthplace of the blues, is also a haven for soulful Southern cooking. In Clarksdale, make your way to Abe's Bar-B-Q (616 N State St, Clarksdale, MS 38614), a local institution since 1924. Their slow-cooked ribs and pulled pork sandwiches, slathered in a tangy barbecue sauce, are legendary.

For a unique dining experience, try Ground Zero Blues Club (387 Delta Ave, Clarksdale, MS 38614), co-owned by actor Morgan Freeman. This spot combines live blues music with hearty Southern dishes like fried catfish and shrimp and grits, providing a feast for both the ears and the stomach.

Coastal Mississippi: Fresh and Flavorful

The Gulf Coast offers a bounty of fresh seafood and vibrant flavors. In Biloxi, Mary Mahoney's Old French House (110 Rue Magnolia, Biloxi, MS 39530) stands out as a historic dining destination. Housed in a building dating back to 1737, it serves exquisite dishes like lobster and crabmeat au gratin.

For a casual seaside meal, head to The Blind Tiger Biloxi Beach (265 Beach Blvd, Biloxi, MS 39530). This beachfront spot offers stunning views and delicious seafood tacos and po'boys. Pair your meal with a refreshing cocktail from their extensive drink menu.

In Gulfport, The Chimneys (1640 E Beach Blvd, Gulfport, MS 39501) is a must-visit for its elegant Southern cuisine. Enjoy dishes like pecan-crusted redfish and shrimp and grits while overlooking the serene Gulf waters.

Oxford: Literary and Culinary Excellence

Oxford, known for its literary heritage, also boasts a vibrant food scene. City Grocery (152 Courthouse Square, Oxford, MS 38655) is a landmark restaurant offering Southern gourmet dishes. Chef John Currence's creations, such as the catfish almondine and braised lamb shank, have earned national acclaim.

For a more laid-back experience, Big Bad Breakfast (719 N Lamar Blvd, Oxford, MS 38655) is the place to be. Serving up hearty Southern breakfast fare like biscuits and gravy, it's the perfect spot to start your day.

Natchez: A Blend of History and Flavor

In Natchez, the culinary scene is as rich as its history. The Carriage House Restaurant (401 High St, Natchez, MS 39120), located in the historic Stanton Hall, offers traditional Southern dishes like fried chicken and shrimp remoulade.

For a unique dining experience, visit Magnolia Grill (49 Silver St, Natchez, MS 39120), which offers stunning views of the Mississippi River. Their menu features a mix of Southern and Creole dishes, including blackened redfish and crawfish étouffée.

Vicksburg: Southern Comfort Foods

In Vicksburg, you'll find comfort foods that warm the soul. Rusty's Riverfront Grill (901 Washington St, Vicksburg, MS 39183) is famous for its seafood platters and steaks. The relaxed atmosphere and river views make it a favorite among locals and visitors alike.

Another gem is Walnut Hills (1214 Adams St, Vicksburg, MS 39183), a historic restaurant offering classic Southern fare. Their fried chicken and homemade pies are must-tries.

Practical Tips for Food Lovers

Plan Ahead: Some popular restaurants can get crowded, so making reservations is a good idea.

Explore Local Markets: Visit farmers' markets for fresh, local produce and homemade goodies.

Try Local Specialties: Don't miss out on regional dishes like Delta tamales, Gulf oysters, and Mississippi mud pie.

Nightlife and Entertainment: Where to Go After Dark

Jackson: The Heart of Mississippi's Nightlife

Jackson, the state capital, offers an eclectic mix of nightlife options. Begin your evening at Hal & Mal's (200 Commerce St, Jackson, MS 39201), a beloved local spot known for its live music and hearty Southern fare. The venue features multiple rooms, each with its own unique vibe, from the intimate Red Room to the bustling Big Room, where you can catch local bands and touring acts.

For a more sophisticated experience, head to The Library Lounge (734 Fairview St, Jackson, MS 39202) located within the historic Fairview Inn. This upscale cocktail bar offers a cozy, book-lined setting perfect for enjoying craft cocktails and light bites. Don't miss their signature drink, the "Writer's Block," a delightful mix of bourbon, amaro, and bitters.

The Mississippi Delta: Where Music Lives

The Delta is renowned as the birthplace of the blues, and its nightlife reflects this rich musical heritage. Ground Zero Blues Club (387 Delta Ave, Clarksdale, MS 38614), co-owned by actor Morgan Freeman, is a must-visit. Located in

Clarksdale, the club offers an authentic blues experience with live performances every night. The rustic setting and lively atmosphere make it a perfect spot to immerse yourself in the Delta's music scene.

Another iconic venue is Red's Lounge (395 Sunflower Ave, Clarksdale, MS 38614), one of the last remaining true juke joints in the Delta. Here, you can experience raw, unfiltered blues music in an intimate, down-home environment.

Coastal Mississippi: Casinos and More

If you're on the Gulf Coast, Biloxi is the place to be for nightlife. The city's numerous casinos offer a mix of gaming, live entertainment, and dining. Beau Rivage Resort & Casino (875 Beach Blvd, Biloxi, MS 39530) is a standout, featuring everything from slot machines and poker tables to live shows and nightclubs. Catch a performance at the Beau Rivage Theatre, which hosts national touring acts and comedy shows.

For a more relaxed evening, visit The Shed Barbeque & Blues Joint (7501 MS-57, Ocean Springs, MS 39565), where you can enjoy live blues music alongside award-winning barbecue. The casual, laid-back atmosphere is perfect for unwinding after a day at the beach.

Oxford: A College Town with a Cultural Twist

Oxford's nightlife is vibrant, thanks in part to its university town atmosphere. Start your night at Proud Larry's (211 S Lamar Blvd, Oxford, MS 38655), a popular spot for live music ranging from local bands to national touring acts. The venue also serves delicious pizzas and a wide selection of beers.

For a more intimate setting, check out The Lyric Oxford (1006 Van Buren Ave, Oxford, MS 38655). This historic theater, originally a silent movie house, now hosts concerts, comedy shows, and other live performances. Its beautifully restored interior adds a touch of elegance to any evening out.

Vicksburg: History and Entertainment

In Vicksburg, you can combine history with nightlife at 10 South Rooftop Bar & Grill (1301 Washington St, Vicksburg, MS 39180). This rooftop bar offers stunning views of the Mississippi River and a relaxed atmosphere perfect for enjoying cocktails and Southern-inspired dishes. The panoramic view is particularly enchanting at sunset.

For live music, visit Ameristar Casino Hotel Vicksburg (4116 Washington St, Vicksburg, MS 39180). Their Bottleneck Blues Bar hosts live blues, rock, and country music in a vibrant setting. The casino floor provides additional entertainment options, from gaming to dining.

Tupelo: Elvis' Hometown

In Tupelo, music is at the heart of the nightlife. Blue Canoe (2006 N Gloster St, Tupelo, MS 38804) is a beloved local hangout offering a mix of live music, craft beers, and delicious food. The venue's eclectic decor and friendly atmosphere make it a favorite among both locals and visitors.

For a more unique experience, visit The Stables Downtown Grill (206 N Spring St, Tupelo, MS 38804). This venue, located in a historic building, features live music and a menu focused on locally sourced ingredients.

Chapter 2: The Mississippi Delta: Birthplace of the Blues

Discovering the Delta's Music Heritage

The Birthplace of the Blues

The Mississippi Delta, stretching from Memphis down to Vicksburg and bordered by the Mississippi and Yazoo rivers, is synonymous with the origins of the blues. It's here that African American musicians, drawing on their cultural heritage and experiences, created a new musical form that would shape the course of modern music.

Clarksdale: Ground Zero for the Blues

No visit to the Delta is complete without a pilgrimage to Clarksdale, often referred to as the "Ground Zero" of the blues. This small town boasts a disproportionate influence on American music. Start your journey at the Delta Blues Museum, housed in a historic freight depot, where exhibits chronicle the lives and legacies of blues legends like Muddy Waters and B.B. King.

Crossroads of Myth and Music

Just outside of Clarksdale, along Highway 61, lies the legendary crossroads where, according to folklore, Robert Johnson sold his soul to the devil in exchange for mastery of the guitar. Although steeped in myth, this intersection symbolizes the Delta's mystique and the profound impact of its musical heritage.

Live Music and Juke Joints

Immerse yourself in the Delta's living musical tradition by visiting its iconic juke joints. These unassuming bars and clubs, often found off the beaten path, offer authentic blues experiences. Ground Zero Blues Club, co-owned by actor Morgan Freeman, stands as a testament to the Delta's enduring musical legacy, hosting live performances that capture the spirit of the blues.

Festivals and Celebrations

Throughout the year, the Delta comes alive with music festivals that celebrate its rich musical heritage. The Juke Joint Festival in Clarksdale attracts thousands of blues enthusiasts with its eclectic lineup of performances, street vendors selling Southern delicacies, and lively atmosphere that embodies the Delta's unique charm.

Exploring Delta History

Beyond music, the Delta offers glimpses into its complex history. Visit Dockery Farms, often considered the birthplace of the blues, where legendary musicians honed their craft amidst the cotton fields. The Mississippi Blues Trail, marked by historical markers across the state, guides visitors through key sites and stories that shaped the blues genre.

Culinary Delights

No exploration of the Delta is complete without savoring its distinctive cuisine. Indulge in Southern comfort foods like fried catfish, collard greens, and cornbread at local eateries that blend traditional flavors with modern twists.

Must-Visit Historical Sites

Vicksburg National Military Park

Located in Vicksburg, this park commemorates one of the most decisive battles of the American Civil War. Visitors can explore over 1,300 monuments and markers, the USS Cairo gunboat, and the Vicksburg National Cemetery. The park's museum provides a comprehensive overview of the siege and battle, highlighting key events and personalities from both sides of the conflict.

Beauvoir, the Jefferson Davis Home and Presidential Library

Situated in Biloxi, Beauvoir was the last home of Jefferson Davis, the President of the Confederate States of America. This historic site includes the beautifully restored antebellum home, museum exhibits detailing Davis's life and career, and a Confederate cemetery. The grounds offer stunning views of the Gulf Coast, providing a serene setting for reflection on the complexities of the Civil War era.

Rowan Oak

In Oxford, visitors can explore Rowan Oak, the former home of Nobel Prize-winning author William Faulkner. This Greek Revival house is set on a picturesque estate and offers guided tours that provide insights into Faulkner's life and writing. The surrounding grounds feature trails that wind through native flora and fauna, creating a tranquil atmosphere that inspired many of Faulkner's literary works.

Longwood

Located in Natchez, Longwood is a striking example of antebellum architecture. This octagonal mansion was designed by Samuel Sloan and was intended to be a luxurious home for cotton planter Haller Nutt. Construction ceased abruptly at the outbreak of the Civil War, leaving the upper floors unfinished. Visitors can tour the completed lower level and gain insight into the lifestyle of wealthy plantation owners in the pre-war South.

Eudora Welty House and Garden

In Jackson, visitors can explore the Eudora Welty House and Garden, the former home of Pulitzer Prize-winning author Eudora Welty. This charming Tudor Revival-style house is preserved much as Welty left it, filled with her personal belongings and literary memorabilia. Guided tours offer a glimpse into Welty's life and writing process, highlighting her profound influence on American literature.

Natchez Trace Parkway

Stretching across 444 miles from Natchez to Nashville, the Natchez Trace Parkway is a scenic route steeped in history. Originally used by Native Americans, European settlers, and traders, the parkway offers numerous historical sites, including prehistoric mounds, pioneer settlements, and Civil War battlefields. Visitors can explore hiking trails, scenic overlooks, and interpretive exhibits that tell the story of the Trace's importance as a major travel route throughout history.

Outdoor Adventures: From Hiking to River Tours

Hiking Trails

Tishomingo State Park: Nestled in the foothills of the Appalachian Mountains, Tishomingo State Park is a haven for hikers. Trails wind through rocky outcroppings, dense forests, and alongside the scenic Bear Creek, offering both challenging hikes and leisurely strolls. Don't miss the famous Swinging Bridge Trail for breathtaking views.

Clark Creek Natural Area: Located near Woodville, Clark Creek Natural Area is renowned for its waterfalls and rugged terrain. The primitive trails take you through deep gorges, past numerous waterfalls, and into lush hardwood forests. It's a perfect spot for photography enthusiasts and those seeking a challenging hike.

Natchez Trace Parkway: This historic route not only offers scenic drives but also boasts several hiking trails that showcase Mississippi's natural beauty. Highlights include the Mount Locust Trail, where you can explore a restored 18th-century inn, and the Jeff Busby Park trails, offering panoramic views of the surrounding countryside.

River Tours

Mississippi River Kayaking: For a truly immersive outdoor experience, consider a kayaking adventure along the mighty Mississippi River. Guided tours are available from various outfitters, allowing you to paddle through serene backwaters, explore hidden coves, and learn about the river's ecological importance and cultural significance.

Pascagoula River: Dubbed the "Singing River" by Native Americans, the Pascagoula River is one of the last free-flowing rivers in the lower 48 states. Join a guided eco-tour to navigate its winding channels, observe diverse wildlife such as alligators and migratory birds, and gain insights into the river's unique ecosystem and conservation efforts.

Tombigbee River: Flowing through northeastern Mississippi, the Tombigbee River offers tranquil settings ideal for leisurely boat tours. Cruise past cypress swamps, historical landmarks like the Old Lock and Dam, and enjoy birdwatching opportunities along the riverbanks. Sunset cruises are particularly popular for capturing stunning views of the Mississippi landscape.

Practical Tips

Seasonal Considerations: Mississippi's climate varies, so check weather conditions before embarking on outdoor adventures. Spring and fall are ideal for hiking due to milder temperatures, while summer offers prime conditions for river tours.

Guided Tours vs. Self-Guided: Depending on your preference and experience level, opt for guided tours for safety and local insights. Many tour operators provide equipment and knowledgeable guides who enhance your outdoor experience.

Permits and Regulations: Some hiking trails and river areas may require permits or have specific regulations. Research in advance and adhere to guidelines to ensure a seamless adventure.

Delta Cuisine: Unique Flavors to Savor

Soulful Staples

1. Fried Catfish

In the Delta, fried catfish isn't just a dish; it's a way of life. Head to local favorites like Doe's Eat Place in Greenville or Lusco's in Greenwood for their legendary catfish platters, served with hushpuppies, coleslaw, and tangy tartar sauce. The secret? Fresh catfish, lightly battered and fried to crispy perfection.

2. Hot Tamales

Believe it or not, the Delta has a long-standing love affair with hot tamales. These spicy treats, a nod to the region's Mexican and African-American influences, are often filled with seasoned beef or pork, wrapped in corn husks, and steamed to perfection. Stop by Abe's Bar-B-Q in Clarksdale or Hicks' World Famous Hot Tamales in Cleveland for an authentic taste.

3. Delta Hot Tamales Trail

For the true tamale aficionado, follow the Delta Hot Tamales Trail, a culinary pilgrimage that winds through small towns and hidden gems. Each stop offers a unique twist on this Delta delicacy, showcasing family recipes passed down through generations.

Farm-to-Table Delights

1. Fresh Gulf Seafood

Although not technically in the Delta, the proximity of the Gulf Coast ensures that Delta restaurants feature some of the freshest seafood around. Indulge in shrimp and grits, oyster po'boys, or crab-stuffed flounder at local haunts like Mary Mahoney's in Biloxi or The Blow Fly Inn in Gulfport.

2. Farm Fresh Produce

The fertile soil of the Delta produces an abundance of fresh produce, from juicy watermelons to succulent peaches and plump tomatoes. Visit farmers' markets in towns like Indianola or Greenwood to sample seasonal delights straight from the field to your plate.

Delta Dining Gems

1. James Beard Award Winners

Believe it or not, the Delta boasts its fair share of James Beard Award-winning chefs and restaurants. Plan a visit to The Crown Restaurant in Indianola, where Chef Johnny Smith combines Southern classics with global influences, or City Grocery in Oxford, known for its innovative take on Delta cuisine.

2. Delta Blues and BBQ

No visit to the Delta is complete without a taste of its famous barbecue. Whether you prefer ribs, pulled pork, or smoked brisket, you'll find mouthwatering BBQ joints throughout the region. Stop by Abe's Bar-B-Q in Clarksdale or The Shed BBQ & Blues Joint in Ocean Springs for finger-licking good BBQ and live blues music.

Sweet Endings

1. Pecan Pie

Round off your Delta dining experience with a slice of homemade pecan pie. Made with locally grown pecans and a buttery crust, this Southern classic is the perfect sweet ending to any meal. Visit The Crown Restaurant in Indianola or Walnut Hills in Vicksburg for a slice of heaven.

2. Delta Sweets Trail

For dessert enthusiasts, the Delta Sweets Trail offers a tantalizing array of treats, from fluffy buttermilk biscuits drizzled with honey to decadent chocolate chess pie. Explore bakeries and cafes in towns like Greenwood and Clarksdale, where every bite tells a story of Southern indulgence.

Experience the Delta

From down-home diners to upscale eateries, the Delta's culinary scene invites you to savor the flavors of Mississippi in every bite. Whether you're a foodie in search of the perfect tamale or a traveler eager to explore the region's rich cultural tapestry, Delta cuisine promises an unforgettable dining experience. Come hungry, leave satisfied, and take home a taste of the Delta with you.

Chapter 3: Coastal Mississippi: Sun, Sand, and Seafood

Beaches and Boardwalks: Top Spots for Sun Seekers

Biloxi Beach

Biloxi Beach stands out as one of the most popular and accessible beach destinations in Coastal Mississippi. With its soft white sands and clear blue waters, it's perfect for families, couples, and solo travelers alike. The beach is complemented by a long boardwalk that runs parallel to the shoreline, offering stunning views and easy access to nearby amenities.

Address: Beach Blvd, Biloxi, MS 39530

Highlights:

Biloxi Lighthouse: A historic landmark dating back to 1848, offering panoramic views of the Gulf Coast.

Casino Row: Adjacent to the beach, where visitors can try their luck at various casinos and enjoy dining and entertainment options.

Gulfport Beach

Just a short drive west from Biloxi lies Gulfport Beach, another gem along the Mississippi Gulf Coast. Known for its wide expanse of sandy shores and gentle waves, Gulfport Beach is ideal for sunbathing, picnicking, and enjoying water sports like jet skiing and parasailing.

Address: Hwy 90, Gulfport, MS 39501

Highlights:

Jones Park: Adjacent to Gulfport Beach, featuring playgrounds, walking paths, and shaded picnic areas.

Island View Casino: A nearby casino with dining options overlooking the beach.

Pass Christian Beach

For those seeking a quieter and more laid-back beach experience, Pass Christian Beach offers a tranquil retreat. This beach is beloved for its natural beauty, calm waters, and scenic views of barrier islands off the coast.

Address: Scenic Dr, Pass Christian, MS 39571

Highlights:

War Memorial Park: A serene park adjacent to the beach, perfect for relaxation and picnicking.

Local Eateries: Nearby restaurants offering fresh seafood and Gulf Coast specialties.

Long Beach

Further west, Long Beach attracts visitors with its long stretch of sandy beachfront and family-friendly atmosphere. This community-oriented beach features a newly renovated boardwalk, perfect for strolling, biking, or simply taking in the views.

Address: Hwy 90, Long Beach, MS 39560

Highlights:

Long Beach Harbor: A bustling hub with shops, restaurants, and a marina offering boat rentals and fishing charters.

Annual Events: Long Beach hosts various festivals and events throughout the year, drawing both locals and tourists alike.

Pascagoula Beach

At the eastern edge of Coastal Mississippi, Pascagoula Beach offers a more secluded and natural beach experience. The beach is known for its calm waters, making it ideal for swimming and paddleboarding, as well as its picturesque sunsets over the Gulf.

Address: Beach Blvd, Pascagoula, MS 39567

Highlights:

Pascagoula River Audubon Center: Nearby nature center offering educational programs and guided tours of local wildlife habitats.

Historic Downtown: Explore Pascagoula's historic district with its charming shops, cafes, and galleries.

Seafood Delights: A Guide to Coastal Dining

Biloxi: A Seafood Lover's Paradise

Start your seafood journey in Biloxi, known for its bustling seafood markets and waterfront eateries. Taranto's Crawfish is a local favorite, where you can indulge in boiled crawfish, shrimp po'boys, and hearty seafood gumbo. For a more upscale experience, head to Mary Mahoney's Old French

House, housed in a historic 1737 building, where their signature seafood platters and crab claws are not to be missed.

Gulfport: Fresh Catches and Ocean Views

Travel east to Gulfport, where seafood restaurants offer stunning views of the Gulf of Mexico. The Reef is a top spot, famous for its laid-back atmosphere and seafood nachos. For a taste of Gulfport's local seafood, Steve's Marina Restaurant is renowned for its seafood platters featuring everything from grilled snapper to buttery crab legs.

Ocean Springs: Artistic Flavors and Culinary Innovation

Venture over to Ocean Springs, where creativity meets culinary excellence. Vestige stands out for its innovative approach to Gulf Coast cuisine, offering dishes like smoked Gulf fish dip and pan-seared scallops with local produce. For a more casual vibe, The Shed BBQ & Blues Joint serves up award-winning barbecue alongside fresh Gulf oysters and shrimp po'boys.

Bay St. Louis: Quaint Charm and Fresh Seafood

Discover Bay St. Louis, where charming eateries beckon with fresh seafood and Southern hospitality. Trapani's Eatery is a must-visit, known for its seafood-stuffed mushrooms and pecan-crusted fish. The Blind Tiger offers a unique dining experience with its waterfront location and specialties like blackened fish tacos and seafood gumbo.

Pass Christian: Historic Eateries and Coastal Cuisine

Wrap up your coastal culinary tour in Pass Christian, a town steeped in history and seafood traditions. Bacchus on the Beach offers panoramic views of the Gulf along with dishes like shrimp and grits and oysters Rockefeller. For a taste of local seafood in a historic setting, Shaggy's Pass Harbor serves up seafood platters and cocktails right on the water's edge.

Casinos and Nightlife: Entertainment by the Gulf

Biloxi: The Casino Capital

Biloxi stands out as the epicenter of casino gaming along the Mississippi Gulf Coast. Nestled right on the waterfront, Biloxi's casinos dazzle with their luxurious settings and round-the-clock excitement. Beau Rivage Casino, a towering presence with its elegant architecture and world-class amenities, sets the stage for a sophisticated evening. Its expansive gaming floor features a variety of table games, slot machines, and poker rooms, ensuring there's always a game to suit your style. The IP Casino Resort Spa offers a more relaxed atmosphere with a focus on entertainment, boasting a state-of-the-art theater hosting top-notch performances and concerts throughout the year.

For those seeking a bit of history with their nightlife, the Golden Nugget Biloxi pays homage to the original Vegas casino, offering a mix of classic charm and modern gaming. Whether you're trying your luck at the tables or catching a live show, the Golden Nugget promises an unforgettable evening.

Gulfport: Casual Vibes and Coastal Charm

A short drive from Biloxi, Gulfport offers a more laid-back yet equally entertaining casino experience. Island View Casino Resort is a local favorite, known for its stunning views of the Gulf and an array of gaming options. From slots to blackjack, the casino floor buzzes with excitement, complemented by live music performances and themed events that keep the energy high.

Bay St. Louis: Quaint Charm with Casino Flair

Venturing further west along the coast, Bay St. Louis combines small-town charm with a dose of casino entertainment. Hollywood Casino is a standout, offering not just gaming but also a taste of Hollywood glamour. The casino features a variety of slots and table games, along with multiple dining options ranging from casual bites to fine dining experiences. The Hollywood Hotel provides a comfortable retreat after a night of gaming and entertainment.

Entertainment Beyond the Tables

Beyond the thrill of gaming, the Gulf Coast casinos offer diverse nightlife experiences. Most casinos host regular live performances by local bands and touring artists, ensuring there's always music to set the mood. Many also feature upscale bars and lounges where you can sip on crafted cocktails while taking in views of the Gulf or enjoying live sports broadcasts.

For a change of pace, the Gulf Coast's nightlife extends beyond the casino walls. Waterfront bars and beachside lounges offer a more relaxed atmosphere, perfect for enjoying a drink as the sun sets over the horizon. Local favorites like The Reef in Biloxi or The Quarter in Gulfport blend coastal charm with lively nightlife, often featuring live music and themed nights that draw both locals and visitors alike.

Nature and Wildlife: Exploring Coastal Preserves

Gulf Islands National Seashore

Location: 3500 Park Road, Ocean Springs, MS 39564

The Gulf Islands National Seashore is a must-visit destination for anyone exploring the Mississippi coast. This expansive preserve encompasses several barrier islands and coastal habitats, offering a pristine environment for outdoor activities. Here, you can hike through pine forests, explore salt marshes, and relax on white sandy beaches. Birdwatchers will delight in the diverse avian species that call this area home, including herons, egrets, and ospreys. The Davis Bayou area, accessible from Ocean Springs, features a visitor center with educational exhibits, hiking trails, and opportunities for kayaking and fishing.

Grand Bay National Estuarine Research Reserve

Location: 6005 Bayou Heron Road, Moss Point, MS 39562

Spanning over 18,000 acres, the Grand Bay National Estuarine Research Reserve is a vital sanctuary for wildlife and a research hub for coastal ecology. Visitors can explore the reserve's varied habitats, including tidal marshes, savannas, and bayous. The interpretive center offers insights into the region's natural history and ongoing research efforts. Don't miss the chance to walk along the boardwalk trails, where you might spot alligators, turtles, and an array of bird species. The reserve also hosts guided tours and educational programs, making it an ideal destination for families and nature enthusiasts.

Pascagoula River Audubon Center

Location: 5107 Arthur Street, Moss Point, MS 39563

The Pascagoula River Audubon Center provides an excellent gateway to explore the Pascagoula River, one of the last free-flowing rivers in the contiguous United States. The center offers interpretive exhibits, a native plant garden, and opportunities for birdwatching. Kayaking and boat tours are available for those who want to delve deeper into the river's winding waterways, where you might encounter dolphins, otters, and a wide variety of bird species. The center's boardwalk trail offers a peaceful stroll through marshland, providing ample opportunities to observe wildlife in their natural habitat.

Ward Bayou Wildlife Management Area

Location: Vancleave, MS 39565 (No physical address; accessed via Poticaw Landing)

Ward Bayou Wildlife Management Area is a hidden gem for those seeking solitude and a closer connection with nature. Covering over 13,000 acres of bottomland hardwood forests, swamps, and bayous, this area is perfect for paddling, fishing, and wildlife observation. The serene waterways of Ward Bayou are ideal for kayaking, offering a chance to see alligators, wading birds, and other wildlife in a tranquil setting. Access the area via Poticaw Landing, and be prepared for a rustic adventure, as facilities are minimal and the area is best suited for experienced outdoor enthusiasts.

Mississippi Sandhill Crane National Wildlife Refuge

Location: 7200 Crane Lane, Gautier, MS 39553

Home to the critically endangered Mississippi Sandhill Crane, this refuge is dedicated to the conservation of this unique bird and its wet pine savanna habitat. The refuge's visitor center provides educational displays and a video presentation about the cranes and the efforts to protect them. Visitors can explore several trails that meander through the refuge, offering glimpses of the cranes and other wildlife such as gopher tortoises and various bird species. The Fontainebleau Trail is a popular choice, providing an easy walk with excellent wildlife viewing opportunities.

Tips for Visiting Coastal Preserves

Plan Ahead: Check the weather forecast and preserve hours before you go. Some areas may have seasonal closures or restricted access due to wildlife conservation efforts.

Pack Essentials: Bring water, snacks, insect repellent, sunscreen, and binoculars for birdwatching.

Respect Wildlife: Maintain a safe distance from all animals, and do not feed or disturb them.

Leave No Trace: Carry out all trash and follow the principles of Leave No Trace to help preserve these natural areas for future generations.

Chapter 4: Oxford and the University Scene

Literary Landmarks: Walking in Faulkner's Footsteps

Rowan Oak: Faulkner's Sanctuary

Address: 916 Old Taylor Road, Oxford, MS 38655

Begin your tour at Rowan Oak, Faulkner's beloved home, where he lived from 1930 until his death in 1962. This Greek Revival house, nestled on 29 acres of woodland, is a tangible link to the author's life and work. As you walk through the rooms, you'll see Faulkner's typewriter, his original manuscripts, and even his handwritten outline for "A Fable" on the walls of his study. The surrounding grounds offer a peaceful retreat, echoing the quiet that Faulkner often sought.

Faulkner's Grave: A Quiet Reflection

Address: St. Peter's Cemetery, 200 N. 16th Street, Oxford, MS 38655

Just a short drive from Rowan Oak, visit St. Peter's Cemetery, where Faulkner is buried. His grave is marked by a simple headstone, often adorned with pens, bottles of whiskey, and other tokens left by admirers. It's a solemn place for reflection on the life and legacy of a literary giant.

Oxford Square: Literary Heartbeat

Address: Courthouse Square, Oxford, MS 38655

Head to the historic Oxford Square, the vibrant center of the town. Here, you'll find Square Books, one of the most renowned independent bookstores in the country.

Square Books

Address: 160 Courthouse Square, Oxford, MS 38655

Square Books has a special section dedicated to Faulkner, featuring first editions, critical studies, and signed copies of his works. The store's balconies offer a perfect spot to enjoy a cup of coffee while reading your latest literary find.

Faulkner Alley: A Hidden Gem

Address: Off the Oxford Square, near 110 Courthouse Square, Oxford, MS 38655

Tucked away near the Oxford Square, you'll find Faulkner Alley, a small, mural-adorned passageway that celebrates the town's literary heritage. It's a great spot for a photo and to ponder the lasting impact of Faulkner's presence in Oxford.

The University of Mississippi: Center for Faulkner Studies

Address: University, MS 38677

The University of Mississippi, affectionately known as Ole Miss, houses the Center for the Study of Southern Culture and the Department of Archives and Special Collections. Here, you can explore extensive collections of Faulkner's manuscripts, letters, and photographs. The annual Faulkner and Yoknapatawpha Conference held at Ole Miss is a must-visit for any serious Faulkner aficionado.

The Lyric Theater: Echoes of Faulkner's Times

Address: 1006 Van Buren Avenue, Oxford, MS 38655

The Lyric Theater, originally a livery stable owned by Faulkner's family, is now a vibrant venue for concerts and events. This historic building connects the past with the present, offering a glimpse into the Oxford that Faulkner knew.

The Faulkner Statue

Address: Outside City Hall, 107 Courthouse Square, Oxford, MS 38655

Outside Oxford's City Hall, you'll find a statue of Faulkner seated on a bench, as if observing the bustling square. It's a fitting tribute to the man who so vividly captured the spirit of this town in his writings.

Staying in Oxford: A Literary Experience

The Graduate Oxford

Address: 400 N. Lamar Boulevard, Oxford, MS 38655

For a true literary experience, stay at The Graduate Oxford, a boutique hotel that pays homage to the town's rich cultural heritage, including nods to Faulkner throughout its decor.

College Town Vibes: Exploring Ole Miss

University of Mississippi: A Campus Like No Other

Address: 1 Grove Loop, University, MS 38677

The University of Mississippi, founded in 1848, is the heart and soul of Oxford. The campus is a harmonious mix of historic buildings and modern facilities, set within beautifully landscaped grounds. The Grove, a ten-acre green space, is the epicenter of student life. On game days, it transforms into one of the most celebrated tailgating spots in college football, where students, alumni, and fans gather for food, fun, and camaraderie.

The Lyceum and Rowan Oak

Address: 1 Grove Loop, University, MS 38677 (The Lyceum)

Address: 916 Old Taylor Rd, Oxford, MS 38655 (Rowan Oak)

The Lyceum, the university's iconic building, stands as a symbol of Ole Miss's rich history. Nearby, Rowan Oak, the historic home of Nobel Prize-winning author William Faulkner, offers a glimpse into the literary heritage of Oxford. Faulkner's influence is deeply ingrained in the town, making it a pilgrimage site for literature enthusiasts.

Oxford Square: The Heartbeat of the Town

Address: Downtown Oxford, MS 38655

Just a short walk from the university, the Oxford Square is the vibrant heart of the town. Lined with boutiques, bookstores, cafes, and restaurants, the Square is the perfect place to soak in the local culture. Square Books, an independent bookstore, is a must-visit for its extensive collection of Southern literature and cozy atmosphere.

Eating Out in Oxford

Oxford's culinary scene is as diverse as it is delicious. From casual eateries to fine dining, there's something for every palate.

Ajax Diner

Address: 118 Courthouse Square, Oxford, MS 38655

A beloved local institution, Ajax Diner serves up hearty Southern comfort food. Their meatloaf, fried catfish, and signature cornbread dressing are crowd favorites.

City Grocery

Address: 152 Courthouse Square, Oxford, MS 38655

For a more upscale dining experience, City Grocery offers a menu that blends Southern flavors with contemporary techniques. The shrimp and grits and the pork chop are standout dishes.

Big Bad Breakfast

Address: 719 N Lamar Blvd, Oxford, MS 38655

Start your day with a visit to Big Bad Breakfast, where you can enjoy classic breakfast fare with a Southern twist. Their biscuits and gravy and the Big Bad Breakfast plate are not to be missed.

Nightlife and Entertainment

Oxford's nightlife is lively and varied, catering to both students and visitors.

The Library Sports Bar

Address: 120 S 11th St, Oxford, MS 38655

A popular hangout for Ole Miss students, The Library Sports Bar offers a lively atmosphere with live music, dance floors, and plenty of big screens for sports enthusiasts.

Proud Larry's

Address: 211 S Lamar Blvd, Oxford, MS 38655

For live music and a laid-back vibe, head to Proud Larry's. This venue hosts an array of local and touring bands, making it a hotspot for music lovers.

Cultural Highlights

Oxford's cultural scene is enriched by the presence of the university and its students.

Ford Center for the Performing Arts

Address: 351 University Ave, University, MS 38677

The Gertrude C. Ford Center for the Performing Arts hosts a variety of performances, including theater, dance, and concerts. It's a hub for cultural activities in the town.

University of Mississippi Museum

Address: University Ave and 5th St, Oxford, MS 38677

This museum features an impressive collection of Southern folk art, Greek and Roman antiquities, and 19th-century scientific instruments. It's a testament to the academic and cultural depth of Ole Miss.

Best Eats: From Cafes to Fine Dining

Jackson: The Capital's Culinary Scene

Walker's Drive-In

3016 N State St, Jackson, MS 39216

Walker's Drive-In combines upscale dining with a relaxed atmosphere. Located in the historic Fondren district, it's known for its creative Southern dishes. Highlights include the Redfish Anna, a grilled fish topped with crabmeat, and the Pecan-Crusted Catfish. The wine list is impressive, making it a perfect spot for a special night out.

Brent's Drugs

655 Duling Ave, Jackson, MS 39216

Step back in time at Brent's Drugs, an old-fashioned soda fountain that has been serving the community since 1946. Enjoy classic diner fare like burgers, milkshakes, and homemade pies. The vintage ambiance adds to the charm, making it a beloved local favorite.

Oxford: Literary and Culinary Delights

City Grocery

152 Courthouse Square, Oxford, MS 38655

Located on the historic Courthouse Square, City Grocery is a cornerstone of Oxford's dining scene. Chef John Currence's menu features Southern-inspired dishes with a modern twist. Don't miss the Shrimp and Grits or the Fried Catfish. The cozy upstairs bar is perfect for a pre-dinner cocktail.

Big Bad Breakfast

719 N Lamar Blvd, Oxford, MS 38655

Also a creation of Chef John Currence, Big Bad Breakfast offers an exceptional start to your day. From fluffy biscuits and gravy to the renowned Big Bad Breakfast Plate, this spot is a must-visit for breakfast lovers. The casual, friendly atmosphere makes it a great place to relax and enjoy a hearty meal.

Coastal Mississippi: Fresh Seafood and More

Mary Mahoney's Old French House

110 Rue Magnolia, Biloxi, MS 39530

Set in a historic house dating back to 1737, Mary Mahoney's is a Gulf Coast institution. The menu is a seafood lover's dream, featuring dishes like Lobster Thermidor and Shrimp and Crabmeat au Gratin. The elegant setting and rich history add to the dining experience, making it a must-visit in Biloxi.

The Shed Barbeque & Blues Joint

7501 MS-57, Ocean Springs, MS 39565

For a more laid-back vibe, head to The Shed. Known for its finger-licking BBQ and live blues music, it's a great spot to unwind and enjoy some Southern hospitality. The pulled pork and ribs are crowd favorites, and the lively atmosphere ensures a fun time.

Delta Delights: Authentic and Soulful

Doe's Eat Place

502 Nelson St, Greenville, MS 38701

Founded in 1941, Doe's Eat Place is a legendary spot in the Delta. Famous for its massive porterhouse steaks and tamales, this no-frills eatery offers a truly authentic taste of Mississippi. The family-style service and rustic setting make it a unique dining experience.

Ground Zero Blues Club

387 Delta Ave, Clarksdale, MS 38614

Co-owned by actor Morgan Freeman, Ground Zero Blues Club is a must-visit for blues enthusiasts and foodies alike. Enjoy live music while savoring Southern favorites like fried green tomatoes and catfish po' boys. The lively atmosphere and rich musical heritage make it a standout spot in Clarksdale.

Natchez: Southern Elegance

The Castle Restaurant & Pub

84 Homochitto St, Natchez, MS 39120

Located in the historic Dunleith mansion, The Castle offers a refined dining experience with a focus on local ingredients. Signature dishes include the Crawfish Étouffée and the Bourbon Pecan Pie. The elegant setting and impeccable service make it perfect for a special occasion.

Mammy's Cupboard

555 US-61, Natchez, MS 39120

Housed in a building shaped like a giant woman, Mammy's Cupboard is a quirky and beloved local eatery. The menu features homemade soups, sandwiches, and desserts, with the homemade pies being particularly popular. The charming and unique atmosphere is sure to leave a lasting impression.

Cultural Highlights: Museums, Art, and Music

Museums

Mississippi Museum of Art (380 S Lamar St, Jackson, MS 39201)

The Mississippi Museum of Art in Jackson is the largest art museum in the state. It houses an impressive collection of over 5,000 works, including pieces by Mississippi artists and an array of American and European masters. Don't miss the New Southern Crossroads exhibit, which explores the intersection of history, culture, and identity in the South.

B.B. King Museum and Delta Interpretive Center (400 Second St, Indianola, MS 38751)

Located in the heart of the Mississippi Delta, the B.B. King Museum celebrates the life and legacy of the blues legend B.B. King. The museum features interactive exhibits, personal memorabilia, and a theater showing documentaries about the Delta blues.

Mississippi Civil Rights Museum (222 North St, Jackson, MS 39201)

This powerful museum chronicles the history of the Civil Rights Movement in Mississippi from 1945 to 1976. Through eight galleries, visitors can experience the struggle for civil rights through photographs, artifacts, and oral histories that bring the past to life.

Art Galleries

Lauren Rogers Museum of Art (565 N 5th Ave, Laurel, MS 39440)

The Lauren Rogers Museum of Art in Laurel is one of the oldest art museums in Mississippi. It features a diverse collection, including American and European paintings, Native American baskets, and Japanese Ukiyo-e woodblock prints. The museum's beautiful Georgian Revival building and peaceful garden add to its charm.

Walter Anderson Museum of Art (510 Washington Ave, Ocean Springs, MS 39564)

Located in Ocean Springs, this museum celebrates the life and work of Walter Anderson, a prolific artist known for his depictions of the Gulf Coast's natural beauty. The museum showcases Anderson's watercolors, block prints, and murals, offering a glimpse into his unique artistic vision.

Music Venues

Ground Zero Blues Club (387 Delta Ave, Clarksdale, MS 38614)

Owned by actor Morgan Freeman, Ground Zero Blues Club is a must-visit for blues enthusiasts. Located in Clarksdale, the club features live performances by some of the best blues musicians in the region. The rustic, juke joint atmosphere adds to the authentic Delta blues experience.

Thalia Mara Hall (255 E Pascagoula St, Jackson, MS 39201)

Thalia Mara Hall in Jackson is the city's premier performing arts center. It hosts a variety of events, including symphony concerts, ballet performances, and Broadway shows. The hall is also home to the USA International Ballet Competition, held every four years.

Blue Front Café (107 E Railroad Ave, Bentonia, MS 39040)

The Blue Front Café in Bentonia is an iconic blues venue and the birthplace of the Bentonia blues style. Founded in 1948 by bluesman Jimmy "Duck" Holmes' parents, the café continues to host live blues performances and is a key stop on the Mississippi Blues Trail.

Cultural Festivals

Natchez Festival of Music (Natchez, MS)

Held annually in May, the Natchez Festival of Music features a diverse lineup of performances, including opera, jazz, and Broadway musicals. The festival celebrates the rich musical heritage of Natchez and draws performers and audiences from across the country.

CelticFest Mississippi (Jackson, MS)

CelticFest, held each September in Jackson, is a celebration of Celtic culture, featuring traditional music, dance, and crafts. The festival includes performances by local and international artists, workshops, and family-friendly activities.

Chapter 5: Vicksburg: History on the River

Civil War Sites: Reliving the Past

Vicksburg National Military Park

Address: 3201 Clay Street, Vicksburg, MS 39183

One of the most famous Civil War sites, the Vicksburg National Military Park, commemorates the campaign, siege, and defense of Vicksburg. This park spans over 1,800 acres and includes 1,325 historic monuments and markers, a 16-mile tour road, a restored Union gunboat, and the Vicksburg National Cemetery. The Siege of Vicksburg, which lasted from May 18 to July 4, 1863, was a critical turning point in the war. Visitors can drive through the park, take guided tours, or walk the battlefield to get a sense of the tactics and sacrifices made. The Visitor Center provides insightful exhibits and a 20-minute film detailing the siege and battle.

Champion Hill Battlefield

Address: 3540 Whitaker Road, Bolton, MS 39041

Located east of Vicksburg, the Champion Hill Battlefield was the site of a crucial battle on May 16, 1863. This encounter was one of the bloodiest of the Vicksburg Campaign and a decisive Union victory. While much of the battlefield is privately owned, some areas are accessible to the public. The Champion Hill Memorial Site and several historical markers provide context and details about the battle. Walking these grounds offers a sobering reflection on the intensity and impact of the conflict.

Grand Gulf Military Park

Address: 12006 Grand Gulf Road, Port Gibson, MS 39150

Grand Gulf Military Park, located near Port Gibson, preserves the history of the Grand Gulf area during the Civil War. The park includes a museum with artifacts from the battle, restored buildings, and the remains of Fort Cobun and Fort Wade. The Battle of Grand Gulf, fought on April 29, 1863, was part of General Ulysses S. Grant's Vicksburg Campaign. Although the Confederates initially repelled the Union forces, the engagement delayed but did not stop Grant's advance towards Vicksburg. The park's serene setting and historical significance make it a must-visit for Civil War enthusiasts.

Jefferson Davis Home and Presidential Library

Address: 2244 Beach Boulevard, Biloxi, MS 39531

Beauvoir, the last home of Jefferson Davis, the President of the Confederate States of America, is located in Biloxi. This historic site includes the beautifully restored Beauvoir mansion, the Jefferson Davis Presidential Library, and the Confederate Cemetery. Guided tours of the mansion offer insights into Davis's life and the Confederate experience during and after the Civil War. The library houses a vast collection of Civil War documents, photographs, and artifacts, providing a comprehensive look at this tumultuous period in American history.

Brice's Crossroads National Battlefield Site

Address: 260 Bethany Road, Baldwyn, MS 38824

Brice's Crossroads National Battlefield Site commemorates the Battle of Brice's Crossroads, a significant Confederate victory under General Nathan Bedford Forrest on June 10, 1864. The battlefield is preserved as a testament to Forrest's tactical genius. Visitors can explore the interpretive center, walk the battlefield, and view several monuments and markers that detail the events of the battle. The site offers a glimpse into the strategies and maneuvers that characterized Civil War battles.

Corinth Civil War Interpretive Center

Address: 501 West Linden Street, Corinth, MS 38834

The Corinth Civil War Interpretive Center is part of the Shiloh National Military Park and provides an in-depth look at the Siege and Battle of Corinth. Corinth was a strategic rail center and the site of two significant battles in 1862. The interpretive center features exhibits, multimedia presentations, and a walking tour that highlights the town's role in the Civil War. The nearby Battery Robinett, a preserved earthwork fortification, further enhances the historical experience.

Riverfront Attractions: What to See and Do

Vicksburg Riverfront Murals

Levee Street, Vicksburg, MS 39180

A stroll along Levee Street reveals the Vicksburg Riverfront Murals, a series of 32 vibrant murals painted on the floodwall. These artworks beautifully depict the city's rich history, from its Native American roots to its pivotal role in the Civil War and beyond. Each mural is accompanied by detailed plaques, making it a self-guided history lesson. The murals are a perfect backdrop for photos and a reflective walk.

Lower Mississippi River Museum

910 Washington Street, Vicksburg, MS 39183

The Lower Mississippi River Museum offers an interactive journey through the history, culture, and ecology of the Mississippi River. Highlights include the restored MV Mississippi IV towboat, where you can explore the pilothouse, engine room, and living quarters. Exhibits cover topics such as river navigation, flood control, and the environmental impact of human activity on the river.

Natchez Under-the-Hill

Silver Street, Natchez, MS 39120

Natchez Under-the-Hill is a historic district along the Natchez riverfront that was once a notorious port known for its rowdy saloons and gamblers. Today, it's a charming area with historic buildings, shops, and restaurants. Key attractions include the Under-the-Hill Saloon, which offers a taste of the past with its rustic decor and lively atmosphere, and the Magnolia Grill, where you can enjoy Southern cuisine with stunning river views.

Natchez Bluff Park

Silver Street, Natchez, MS 39120

Perched high above the Mississippi River, Natchez Bluff Park provides panoramic views of the river and surrounding landscape. It's an ideal spot for a leisurely walk, a picnic, or simply soaking in the sunset. The park also features historical markers and monuments that highlight Natchez's significance as a port city.

Grand Village of the Natchez Indians

400 Jefferson Davis Boulevard, Natchez, MS 39120

For a deeper dive into the region's pre-colonial history, visit the Grand Village of the Natchez Indians. This 128-acre site includes a reconstructed Natchez Indian house, three ceremonial mounds, and a museum with artifacts and exhibits. The village offers a glimpse into the lives and culture of the Natchez people, who inhabited the area long before European settlers arrived.

Greenville Riverfront

Main Street, Greenville, MS 38701

Greenville's riverfront area has undergone significant revitalization, transforming it into a lively destination with a blend of recreational and cultural attractions. The Greenville History Museum, located nearby at 409 Washington Avenue, offers fascinating exhibits on local history. The riverfront itself features parks, walking trails, and the E.E. Bass Cultural Arts Center, which hosts art exhibits, performances, and community events.

Tunica RiverPark & Museum

1 River Park Drive, Tunica, MS 38676

The Tunica RiverPark & Museum offers an immersive experience of the Mississippi River's natural and cultural heritage. The museum's exhibits cover river ecology, the history of river transport, and the impact of the river on local communities. Outside, the riverwalk trails provide scenic views, and the Tunica Queen riverboat offers cruises that allow visitors to experience the river up close.

Local Cuisine: Southern Comfort Foods

Jackson: A Culinary Journey

In Jackson, the state capital, you'll find a variety of eateries that celebrate Southern comfort food with a local twist.

Bulldog Burger Company

4500 I-55 North, Suite 244, Jackson, MS 39211

This casual spot serves up some of the best burgers in the state, made from fresh, locally sourced ingredients. Try their signature Bulldog Burger, topped with bacon, cheddar, and a fried egg.

Big Apple Inn

448 N Farish St, Jackson, MS 39202

A historic staple in Jackson, this unassuming eatery is famous for its pig ear sandwiches and smoked sausage sandwiches, offering a taste of authentic Southern cuisine.

The Mississippi Delta: Unique Flavors

The Delta region is renowned for its rich culinary heritage, particularly its contributions to the world of barbecue and soul food.

Abe's Bar-B-Q

616 N State St, Clarksdale, MS 38614

Abe's has been serving up legendary barbecue since 1924. Their pulled pork sandwiches and smoked ribs are a must-try, paired with their signature Delta-style sauce.

The Crown Restaurant

614 Delta Ave, Indianola, MS 38751

Known for its Southern hospitality, The Crown offers delightful dishes like Delta catfish and pecan pie. Their hot tamales, a local specialty, are a standout.

Coastal Mississippi: Seafood Delights

The Gulf Coast is a seafood lover's paradise, where fresh catches are transformed into delectable dishes.

Mary Mahoney's Old French House

110 Rue Magnolia, Biloxi, MS 39530

Housed in a building dating back to 1737, Mary Mahoney's offers a charming dining experience with dishes like stuffed flounder and shrimp étouffée, capturing the essence of Gulf Coast cuisine.

The Shed BBQ & Blues Joint

7501 MS-57, Ocean Springs, MS 39565

A lively spot known for its barbecue, The Shed also serves up fantastic Gulf shrimp and smoked sausage, offering a true taste of Coastal Mississippi.

Oxford and the University Scene: Southern Charm

Oxford, home to the University of Mississippi, combines college-town energy with Southern culinary traditions.

Ajax Diner

118 Courthouse Square, Oxford, MS 38655

Located on the historic Square, Ajax Diner is beloved for its down-home dishes like meatloaf, fried catfish, and squash casserole. Their sweet tea and banana pudding are also not to be missed.

City Grocery

152 Courthouse Square, Oxford, MS 38655

An upscale Southern bistro, City Grocery features dishes like shrimp and grits and fried oysters, blending traditional flavors with contemporary flair.

Natchez: Antebellum Splendor

Natchez, known for its antebellum homes, also boasts a rich culinary scene.

The Carriage House Restaurant

401 High St, Natchez, MS 39120

Situated in the historic Stanton Hall, this restaurant offers Southern classics such as fried chicken, cornbread, and greens. Dining here feels like stepping back in time.

King's Tavern

613 Jefferson St, Natchez, MS 39120

One of the oldest buildings in Natchez, King's Tavern serves wood-fired flatbreads and craft cocktails. Their dishes, like braised short ribs, showcase local ingredients and traditional recipes.

Vicksburg: Riverfront Dining

In Vicksburg, you'll find comfort food with a view of the mighty Mississippi River.

Walnut Hills

1214 Adams St, Vicksburg, MS 39183

Known for its round table communal dining, Walnut Hills offers Southern staples such as fried chicken, turnip greens, and homemade biscuits in a charming historic setting.

Rusty's Riverfront Grill

901 Washington St, Vicksburg, MS 39183

With a menu featuring fresh seafood and steaks, Rusty's is a local favorite. Their crab cakes and fried green tomatoes are highly recommended.

Shopping and Souvenirs: Where to Find Unique Gifts

Jackson

Fondren District

The Fondren District in Jackson is a vibrant area filled with eclectic shops and boutiques. Visit The Beagle Bagel Cafe (4500 I-55 North, Jackson, MS 39211) for a local twist on shopping with freshly baked goods and a selection of Mississippi-made products. Another gem is Fondren Corner (2906 N State St, Jackson, MS 39216), where you'll find a mix of art galleries, clothing stores, and gift shops.

Lemuria Books

Located at 4465 I-55 North, Jackson, MS 39206, Lemuria Books is a beloved independent bookstore offering a fantastic selection of signed first editions, Mississippi authors, and a cozy atmosphere perfect for browsing. Their knowledgeable staff can help you find the perfect book or gift.

Oxford

Square Books

At 160 Courthouse Square, Oxford, MS 38655, Square Books is an iconic bookstore in the heart of Oxford's downtown square. With an impressive collection of literature, particularly works by Mississippi authors like William Faulkner, this bookstore is a must-visit for book lovers.

The Mustard Seed Antique Mall

Located at 1903 University Ave, Oxford, MS 38655, this antique mall is a treasure trove of vintage finds, from classic furniture to unique collectibles. Each booth offers something different, ensuring a varied and exciting shopping experience.

Vicksburg

The Attic Gallery

This charming gallery, located at 1101 Washington St, Vicksburg, MS 39183, showcases Southern contemporary art, folk art, and handmade crafts. It's the perfect place to pick up a unique piece of art or a handcrafted gift.

Vicksburg Old Town

Stroll through Vicksburg's historic downtown area, where you'll find a variety of shops offering antiques, local crafts, and Civil War memorabilia. Lorelei Books (1103 Washington St, Vicksburg, MS 39183) is a notable spot for history buffs and literary enthusiasts.

Natchez

Silver Street Gallery & Gifts

At 504 Silver St, Natchez, MS 39120, this shop offers a curated selection of local art, handmade jewelry, and unique gifts. It's located in the historic Natchez Under-the-Hill area, adding to its charm.

Nest

Located at 505 Franklin St, Natchez, MS 39120, Nest is a delightful boutique offering home decor, gifts, and clothing. The shop features a mix of vintage and contemporary items, making it a great place to find something special.

Coastal Mississippi

Lazy Magnolia Brewery

For a taste of local flavor, visit Lazy Magnolia Brewery at 7030 Roscoe Turner Rd, Kiln, MS 39556. The brewery offers tours and tastings, and their gift shop is stocked with unique beer-related merchandise and souvenirs.

Shearwater Pottery

Located at 102 Shearwater Dr, Ocean Springs, MS 39564, Shearwater Pottery has been creating beautiful, handcrafted pottery since 1928. Each piece is unique and reflects the artistic heritage of the region.

Tupelo

Tupelo Hardware Company

A historic hardware store located at 114 W Main St, Tupelo, MS 38804, Tupelo Hardware Company is famous for being the place where Elvis Presley's mother bought his first guitar. The store offers a variety of tools, hardware, and Elvis memorabilia.

Reed's Department Store

Located at 118 W Main St, Tupelo, MS 38804, Reed's is a family-owned department store that has been serving the community since 1905. It offers a range of clothing, gifts, and home goods, making it a great spot for unique finds

Chapter 6: Natchez: Southern Charm and Antebellum Splendor

Antebellum Homes: A Step Back in Time

Natchez: A Hub of Antebellum Splendor

Natchez, perched on the bluffs overlooking the Mississippi River, boasts the largest collection of antebellum homes in the South. Strolling down Natchez's tree-lined streets feels like a journey through time, with over 1,000 structures listed on the National Register of Historic Places. Homes like Longwood, a striking octagonal mansion left unfinished due to the Civil War, or Stanton Hall, known for its Greek Revival architecture and opulent interiors, offer glimpses into the lives of the Southern elite.

Vicksburg: Echoes of History

In Vicksburg, the antebellum homes offer a different perspective, deeply intertwined with the city's Civil War history. Cedar Grove Mansion, with its blend of Greek Revival and Italianate styles, stands as a testament to

Vicksburg's resilience and architectural prowess. Beyond its ornate facades and lush gardens, Cedar Grove provides a poignant reminder of Vicksburg's role in shaping American history.

Natchez Trace Parkway: Hidden Gems

Venturing along the Natchez Trace Parkway unveils lesser-known but equally captivating antebellum homes. Places like Mount Locust, an inn dating back to the late 1700s and now a living museum, offer a glimpse into the daily life of travelers along the historic trace. Further along the parkway, the allure of preserved homes such as Windsor Ruins, with its haunting columns rising from the earth, captures the imagination with tales of grandeur lost to time.

Preservation Efforts and Community

Preserving these homes is a labor of love for Mississippians, reflecting a commitment to honoring their cultural heritage. Many estates, such as the Rosalie Mansion in Natchez, now serve as museums and event venues, welcoming visitors to explore their ornate interiors and lush gardens. The dedication of local preservation societies ensures that these architectural treasures remain accessible, providing educational opportunities and enriching the community's understanding of its past.

Experience and Reflection

Visiting Mississippi's Antebellum homes is not just about admiring architecture; it's about connecting with the stories embedded in their walls. It's about understanding the complexities of Southern history, from the opulence of plantation life to the hardships endured by enslaved communities. These homes offer a nuanced perspective, inviting reflection on the legacies of the past and their impact on contemporary Southern culture.

Riverboat Cruises: Exploring the Mighty Mississippi

Natchez Riverboat Cruises

Natchez, renowned for its antebellum architecture and Southern charm, is an ideal starting point for exploring the Mississippi River. Several companies operate riverboat cruises here, each offering its unique blend of history and hospitality.

1. Natchez Steamboat

The Natchez Steamboat, an authentic steam-powered paddlewheeler, is a staple of the Natchez riverfront. Embarking from the Natchez Under-the-Hill area, this boat offers daily cruises that showcase the city's historical landmarks and natural beauty. As you glide along the river, the captain narrates tales of the area's past, from its Native American heritage to its pivotal role in the Civil War.

2. Dinner Cruises

For a more luxurious experience, consider a dinner cruise aboard one of Natchez's riverboats. These cruises combine fine dining with panoramic views of the river and its surroundings. Enjoy Southern specialties like gumbo and pecan pie while live jazz music fills the air, creating a memorable evening under the stars.

Vicksburg Riverfront Excursions

Vicksburg, steeped in Civil War history, offers a different perspective on Mississippi River cruises. Riverfront excursions here often focus on the city's military past and its strategic importance during the Civil War.

1. Vicksburg Battlefield Tours

Many riverboat cruises in Vicksburg include tours of the Vicksburg National Military Park. From the river, you can see the bluffs and forts that played a crucial role in the Siege of Vicksburg. Knowledgeable guides provide insights into the battles and strategies that shaped American history.

2. Sunset Cruises

For a more leisurely experience, opt for a sunset cruise along the Vicksburg riverfront. These cruises offer stunning views of the Mississippi at dusk, with the setting sun casting a golden glow over the water. It's a perfect opportunity to relax and reflect on the day's explorations.

Mississippi Delta River Adventures

In the Mississippi Delta, where the blues were born, riverboat cruises offer a blend of music, culture, and natural splendor. Departing from towns like Greenville and Clarksdale, these cruises delve into the region's rich musical heritage and agricultural landscapes.

1. Blues and Heritage Cruises

Some riverboat operators in the Delta specialize in blues-themed cruises. Live music performances aboard the boat bring the Delta blues to life, with musicians sharing stories and songs that echo the soulful rhythms of the region.

2. Eco-Tours and Wildlife Viewing

For nature enthusiasts, eco-tours along the Mississippi Delta focus on the area's diverse wildlife and ecosystems. Spot bald eagles, alligators, and other native species as you navigate through the Delta's backwaters and swamps.

Practical Tips for Riverboat Cruises

Booking: It's advisable to book riverboat cruises in advance, especially during peak tourist seasons.

Attire: Casual attire is generally appropriate, but for dinner cruises, smart casual or business casual attire is recommended.

Photography: Don't forget your camera or smartphone to capture the stunning landscapes and historic sites along the river.

Weather: Check the weather forecast before your cruise and dress accordingly, as conditions on the river can be breezy even during warmer months.

Festivals and Events: Year-Round Celebrations

Spring

Double Decker Arts Festival (Oxford)

Taking place in late April, the Double Decker Arts Festival in Oxford is a celebration of art, music, and food. Named after the city's iconic double-decker bus imported from England, the festival features over 100 art vendors, live music stages showcasing local and regional talent, and a variety of food vendors offering Southern delicacies and international cuisine.

Natchez Spring Pilgrimage (Natchez)

Historic homes open their doors to visitors during the Natchez Spring Pilgrimage, held in March and April. This event allows guests to tour beautifully preserved antebellum homes, interact with costumed guides who bring history to life, and enjoy evening concerts and performances that highlight Natchez's rich cultural heritage.

Summer

Mississippi Firefly Festival (Vicksburg)

In June, the Mississippi Firefly Festival illuminates the night with its enchanting display of fireflies along the banks of the Mississippi River. Families and nature enthusiasts gather to observe these magical creatures and participate in activities such as storytelling, live music, and local food offerings.

Gulf Coast Summer Fest Jazz Edition (Biloxi)

Jazz enthusiasts flock to Biloxi in August for the Gulf Coast Summer Fest Jazz Edition. This event features world-class jazz musicians performing at the picturesque Jones Park, overlooking the Gulf of Mexico. Attendees can enjoy not only the music but also local seafood, arts and crafts vendors, and activities for all ages.

Fall

Mississippi Delta Blues & Heritage Festival (Greenville)

Held in September, the Mississippi Delta Blues & Heritage Festival is a must-attend event for music lovers. Celebrating the birthplace of the blues, this festival showcases both legendary performers and up-and-coming artists on multiple stages. Visitors can also enjoy Southern cuisine, arts and crafts, and workshops on the history and culture of the blues.

Mississippi State Fair (Jackson)

Every October, the Mississippi State Fair transforms the state fairgrounds in Jackson into a bustling carnival of rides, games, livestock exhibits, and live entertainment. Families come together to enjoy classic fair foods like funnel cakes and corn dogs, thrilling rides, and nightly concerts featuring popular musicians.

Winter

Victorian Candlelit Christmas (Natchez)

During December, Natchez transports visitors back in time with its Victorian Candlelit Christmas celebration. Historic homes adorned with holiday decorations open their doors for candlelit tours, offering glimpses into Christmas traditions of the 19th century. Festivities include carriage rides, caroling, and seasonal treats.

Christmas on Ice (Biloxi)

Biloxi's Christmas on Ice, held from late November through December, transforms the Mississippi Coast Coliseum into a winter wonderland. Visitors can skate on an indoor ice rink, visit Santa's village, enjoy holiday-themed performances, and marvel at the spectacular ice sculptures on display.

Ongoing Events

Mississippi Pecan Festival (Richton)

This annual festival in September celebrates the state's pecan industry with arts and crafts vendors, live music, pecan-themed food offerings, and activities for all ages.

Great Mississippi River Balloon Race (Natchez)

Each October, the Great Mississippi River Balloon Race fills the skies over Natchez with colorful hot air balloons. The event features balloon races and glows, live music, a balloon glow run, and a children's carnival.

Dining and Nightlife: Best Spots to Eat and Drink

Jackson

In Jackson, the capital city, dining options range from casual diners to upscale eateries. For a taste of local flavor, visit The Iron Horse Grill, housed in a historic train depot, known for its Southern classics like fried green tomatoes and catfish po'boys. Babalu Tacos & Tapas in Fondren is perfect for those craving Latin-inspired dishes and creative cocktails.

For a night out, head to Hal & Mal's, a legendary spot featuring live music and a relaxed atmosphere. Craft beer enthusiasts should check out Lucky Town Brewing Company for its local brews and laid-back vibe.

Coastal Mississippi

Along the Gulf Coast, seafood takes center stage. Mary Mahoney's Old French House in Biloxi is celebrated for its seafood gumbo and shrimp étouffée, served in a charming 18th-century house. The Reef, located right on the beach in Biloxi, offers stunning views and a diverse menu that includes everything from fresh seafood to juicy steaks.

For nightlife, IP Casino Resort Spa in Biloxi offers not only gaming but also multiple bars and restaurants, ensuring a lively evening. The Shed BBQ & Blues Joint in Ocean Springs is a must-visit for BBQ enthusiasts, featuring live blues music and a welcoming, down-home atmosphere.

Oxford

Oxford, home to the University of Mississippi, boasts a lively culinary scene influenced by its literary heritage. City Grocery is an iconic spot known for its elevated Southern cuisine and inventive cocktails. Snackbar, a cozy eatery nearby, offers small plates and craft cocktails in a relaxed setting.

After dinner, head to The Library, a historic bar known for its extensive whiskey selection and live music performances. Proud Larry's is another favorite, offering a laid-back atmosphere with live music and a great selection of local beers.

Natchez

In Natchez, dining often revolves around historic settings and Southern hospitality. The Castle Restaurant & Pub offers fine dining in an antebellum mansion with sweeping views of the Mississippi River. Biscuits & Blues serves up hearty Southern breakfasts and lunches with live blues music in the evenings.

For a nightcap, visit King's Tavern, one of the oldest buildings in Natchez, for craft cocktails and a cozy atmosphere. The Camp Restaurant & Bar is another local favorite, offering a lively ambiance with outdoor seating and live entertainment.

Vicksburg

Vicksburg blends history with modern dining experiences. Walnut Hills Restaurant & Tavern is famous for its Southern buffet and historic ambiance. Cottonwood Public House offers craft beers and Southern-inspired dishes in a relaxed setting.

For nightlife, 10 South Rooftop Bar & Grill provides stunning views of the Mississippi River and a diverse menu of cocktails and small bites. Roca Restaurant & Bar offers a sophisticated dining experience with a vibrant bar scene.

Delta Region

In the Delta, dining experiences often celebrate the region's rich musical heritage and agricultural roots. The Crown Restaurant in Indianola is a local institution known for its steaks and Southern specialties. Ground Zero Blues Club in Clarksdale offers a true Delta blues experience with live music and hearty Southern fare.

Chapter 7: The Natchez Trace Parkway: Scenic Drives and Hidden Gems

Top Scenic Stops: Must-See Points of Interest

1. Mount Locust Historic Site

Located near Natchez, Mount Locust is the only surviving inn on the Trace. This restored 18th-century inn offers a glimpse into pioneer life and serves as a starting point for understanding the area's rich history.

2. Cypress Swamp

Just south of Tupelo, the Cypress Swamp offers a serene experience with its ancient trees draped in Spanish moss. Take a leisurely stroll on the boardwalk and marvel at the tranquil waters reflecting the lush greenery above.

3. Tishomingo State Park

Nestled in the foothills of the Appalachian Mountains, Tishomingo State Park is a haven for outdoor enthusiasts. Explore its unique rock formations, winding creeks, and diverse wildlife. Don't miss a hike along the Bear Creek Canyon Trail for breathtaking views.

4. Jeff Busby Park

Perched atop the highest point on the Trace, Jeff Busby Park offers panoramic vistas of the surrounding countryside. It's an ideal spot for picnicking, birdwatching, or simply taking in the expansive views from the observation tower.

5. French Camp Historic Village

Step back in time at French Camp, a living history village showcasing early American pioneer life. Wander through restored cabins, visit the historic Presbyterian Church, and learn about the area's role in the settlement of the Mississippi frontier.

6. Natchez Trace Parkway Visitor Center

Located near Tupelo, this visitor center is an excellent starting point for your journey. Discover exhibits on the natural and cultural history of the Trace, pick up maps and brochures, and get insider tips from park rangers.

7. Emerald Mound

One of the largest Native American mounds in the United States, Emerald Mound is a marvel of ancient engineering.

Explore the terraces and learn about the indigenous people who built and inhabited this impressive site centuries ago.

8. Ross Barnett Reservoir

Near Jackson, Ross Barnett Reservoir offers a picturesque setting for boating, fishing, and relaxation. Take a scenic drive along the Natchez Trace or stop for a picnic with views of the shimmering waters and surrounding woodlands.

9. Pharr Mounds

These ancient burial mounds near Tupelo provide a glimpse into Mississippi's prehistoric past. Wander among the carefully preserved mounds and imagine life in this area thousands of years ago.

10. Meriwether Lewis Monument and Gravesite

Pay homage to the famed explorer at his monument and gravesite near Hohenwald, Tennessee. Learn about his role in the Lewis and Clark Expedition and reflect on his legacy while enjoying the peaceful surroundings.

Outdoor Activities: Hiking, Biking, and More

Hiking Trails

Mississippi boasts an array of hiking trails that cater to varying skill levels and interests. One standout destination is Tishomingo State Park, located in the northeastern part of the state. Here, you can hike along rocky outcroppings, through lush forests, and alongside the winding Bear Creek. The Bear Creek Canyon Trail is a favorite, offering breathtaking views of the park's unique rock formations and clear streams.

For those interested in coastal landscapes, the Gulf Islands National Seashore offers several trails that wind through marshes, pine forests, and along pristine beaches. The Davis Bayou Trail, near Ocean Springs, provides a glimpse into coastal ecosystems and birdwatching opportunities.

Biking Routes

Cyclists will find plenty to love in Mississippi, with diverse biking routes that showcase the state's scenic beauty. The Natchez Trace Parkway is a renowned cycling route that stretches through Mississippi, offering cyclists a chance to ride along a historic corridor dotted with scenic overlooks and ancient Native American mounds. The gently rolling terrain and low traffic make it ideal for both beginners and experienced riders alike.

In the northern part of the state, the Tanglefoot Trail stretches for 44 miles from Houston to New Albany, following the path of a former railroad line. This trail passes through charming small towns, rural landscapes, and offers amenities such as bike rentals and rest stops along the way.

Other Outdoor Adventures

Beyond hiking and biking, Mississippi offers a variety of other outdoor activities. Canoeing and kayaking enthusiasts can explore the state's numerous waterways, including the scenic Black Creek in southern Mississippi, known for its clear waters and cypress trees. The Pascagoula River, often called the "Singing River" by locals, offers opportunities for paddling through tranquil waters amidst a rich diversity of wildlife.

For those seeking a more adventurous experience, the Mississippi Gulf Coast provides opportunities for fishing charters, sailing excursions, and even dolphin-watching tours. Charter companies operate out of Biloxi and Gulfport, offering guided trips into the Gulf of Mexico or along the Intracoastal Waterway.

Historical Landmarks: Tracing the Past

Vicksburg National Military Park stands as a solemn testament to one of the Civil War's most decisive battles. Located on the bluffs overlooking the Mississippi River, this park preserves the battlefield where Union forces under General Ulysses S. Grant besieged Confederate troops led by General John C. Pemberton. Visitors can explore over 1,300 monuments, markers, and memorials, each honoring the soldiers who fought and died here. The park's visitor center provides comprehensive exhibits and interpretive programs that vividly recount the events of the siege.

In Natchez, a city famed for its opulent antebellum architecture, the Longwood Estate stands out. This unfinished octagonal mansion, with its distinctive onion-shaped dome, offers a rare glimpse into the pre-Civil War Southern plantation life. Visitors can tour the lavishly decorated rooms and learn about the tragic tale of its construction halted by the outbreak of the Civil War.

The Windsor Ruins, near Port Gibson, are another poignant reminder of the South's grandeur and its eventual devastation. Only 23 of the original 29 columns remain standing from what was once the largest antebellum Greek Revival mansion in the state. The ruins evoke a sense of awe and reflection, surrounded by the serene beauty of rural Mississippi.

Further north, Tupelo honors its most famous native son at the Elvis Presley Birthplace and Museum. This humble two-room house, where the King of Rock 'n' Roll was born in 1935, now serves as a museum showcasing Presley's early life and career. The museum complex includes a chapel, a memorial garden, and exhibits tracing Elvis's rise to stardom.

Meridian boasts the Meridian Union Station and Museum, a beautifully restored train station dating back to 1906. Once a bustling hub of transportation, it now houses exhibits detailing Meridian's railroad history and its role in shaping the region's economy.

Chapter 8: Small Town Treasures

Discovering Mississippi's Quaintest Towns

Bay St. Louis

Nestled along the picturesque Gulf Coast, Bay St. Louis is a gem known for its artistic vibe and scenic waterfront views. The historic Old Town area boasts charming shops, art galleries, and cafes housed in colorful cottages. Visitors can stroll along the beachfront promenade, explore local art studios, and enjoy fresh seafood at waterfront restaurants. Don't miss the Second Saturday Artwalk, where local artists showcase their work amidst live music and vibrant street scenes.

Address: Bay St. Louis, MS 39520

Oxford

Home to the University of Mississippi (Ole Miss), Oxford combines Southern hospitality with literary heritage. The town square, surrounded by antebellum architecture and shaded by centuries-old oak trees, invites leisurely walks and boutique shopping experiences. Literary enthusiasts can visit Rowan Oak, the former home of Nobel Prize-winning author William Faulkner. Oxford's vibrant food scene ranges from upscale dining to cozy Southern eateries, offering a taste of authentic Mississippi cuisine.

Address: Oxford, MS 38655

Natchez

Perched on the bluffs overlooking the Mississippi River, Natchez is renowned for its well-preserved antebellum homes and Southern hospitality. Historic tours take visitors through grand estates like Longwood and Stanton Hall, offering a glimpse into the opulent lifestyle of the Old South. The Natchez Trace Parkway, a scenic route through rolling hills and forests, beckons outdoor enthusiasts with hiking trails and picturesque picnic spots. Natchez also hosts annual festivals celebrating its cultural heritage, including the Natchez Balloon Festival and Spring Pilgrimage.

Address: Natchez, MS 39120

Clarksdale

Located in the heart of the Mississippi Delta, Clarksdale is synonymous with the birthplace of the blues. Visitors can explore iconic blues landmarks such as the Delta Blues

Museum and Ground Zero Blues Club, where live music fills the air nightly. The town's rustic charm extends to its juke joints and soul food eateries, where locals and tourists alike gather to savor traditional Southern dishes. Clarksdale's annual Juke Joint Festival attracts blues enthusiasts from around the world, celebrating the genre's enduring legacy.

Address: Clarksdale, MS 38614

Ocean Springs

Set against the backdrop of the Biloxi Bay, Ocean Springs offers a blend of coastal beauty and artistic flair. The town's quaint downtown area is lined with galleries, boutiques, and cafes, showcasing local artwork and crafts. Live oaks draped with Spanish moss provide shade in the town's parks and along its scenic waterfront promenade. Visitors can explore historic sites like the Walter Anderson Museum of Art, dedicated to the renowned local artist, or enjoy outdoor activities such as kayaking in the bay and hiking in nearby nature preserves.

Address: Ocean Springs, MS 39564

Unique Festivals and Local Events

Mississippi Festivals and Local Events

1. Natchez Spring Pilgrimage

Location: Natchez, MS

Date: March-April (dates vary annually)

Description: This historic event allows visitors to tour antebellum homes and gardens that are usually closed to the public. It's a showcase of Natchez's rich history and architectural beauty, featuring guided tours, performances, and special events.

2. Mississippi Delta Blues & Heritage Festival

Location: Greenville, MS

Date: September

Description: Held annually since 1978, this festival celebrates the birthplace of the blues. It brings together legendary blues musicians, local artists, and visitors from around the world for a weekend of soulful music, food, and storytelling.

3. Neshoba County Fair

Location: Philadelphia, MS

Date: July-August (first week)

Description: Known as "Mississippi's Giant House Party," this week-long fair is a cherished tradition. It features horse racing, agricultural exhibits, arts and crafts, and political speeches, making it a unique blend of entertainment and cultural heritage.

4. World Catfish Festival

Location: Belzoni, MS

Date: April

Description: This festival celebrates Belzoni's title as the "Catfish Capital of the World." Visitors can enjoy live music, arts and crafts, and of course, delicious catfish dishes prepared in various Southern styles.

5. Mississippi Pecan Festival

Location: Richton, MS

Date: September-October (dates vary annually)

Description: Celebrating the pecan harvest, this festival features pecan-related foods, arts and crafts, music, and activities for the whole family. It's a great way to experience Mississippi's agricultural heritage.

6. Double Decker Arts Festival

Location: Oxford, MS

Date: April

Description: Named after Oxford's famous double-decker bus imported from England, this festival showcases local and regional artists, musicians, and food vendors. It's a lively event that attracts thousands of visitors each year.

7. Great Mississippi River Balloon Race

Location: Natchez, MS

Date: October

Description: This three-day event features hot air balloon races along the Mississippi River, as well as live music, arts and crafts, and food vendors. It's a spectacular sight to see colorful balloons floating against the backdrop of the river.

8. Mississippi Songwriters Festival

Location: Ocean Springs, MS

Date: September

Description: Held on the Gulf Coast, this festival celebrates the art of songwriting with performances by local and national songwriters. It's a unique opportunity to discover new music and enjoy the coastal ambiance.

9. Tupelo Elvis Festival

Location: Tupelo, MS

Date: June

Description: Celebrating Tupelo's most famous native, this festival features Elvis tribute artists, concerts, a parade, and a variety of Elvis-themed activities. It's a must-visit for fans of the King of Rock 'n' Roll.

10. Mississippi State Fair

Location: Jackson, MS

Date: October

Description: One of the largest fairs in the state, the Mississippi State Fair offers rides, agricultural exhibits, live entertainment, and a wide variety of food vendors. It's a fun-filled event for families and visitors of all ages.

Regional Cuisines: From BBQ to Biscuits

Barbecue (BBQ):

Barbecue in Mississippi isn't just a meal; it's a way of life. Whether you find yourself in the heart of Jackson or a small town along Highway 61, the aroma of slow-smoked meats will draw you in. Each region boasts its own style: in the Delta, you'll savor tender pulled pork drenched in tangy vinegar-based sauce, while in the Pine Belt, ribs are slathered in a sweet molasses glaze. Local favorites include The Shed BBQ & Blues Joint in Ocean Springs, known for its award-winning ribs and lively atmosphere, and The Pig & Pint in Jackson, where craft beer pairs perfectly with smoked brisket and homemade sides.

Southern Comfort Foods:

When it comes to comfort food, Mississippians excel in creating dishes that warm the soul. Head to The Crystal Grill in Greenwood for a taste of their famous chicken fried steak with creamy mashed potatoes and gravy, or stop by Ajax Diner in Oxford for a plate of crispy fried catfish served with hushpuppies and coleslaw. Don't miss the chance to try a plate lunch—a Southern tradition featuring hearty portions of meat, vegetables, and cornbread—at local gems like Mama Hamil's in Madison, where generations have gathered for fried chicken and okra stew.

Biscuits and Gravy:

Breakfast in Mississippi is incomplete without biscuits and gravy. From flaky buttermilk biscuits to savory sausage gravy, this beloved dish can be found on breakfast tables across the state. For a taste of tradition, visit Big Bad Breakfast in Oxford, where biscuits are made from scratch daily and served alongside country ham and creamy sausage gravy. In Tupelo, Connie's Fried Chicken serves up their biscuits with a side of golden-fried chicken, creating a perfect blend of flavors that locals and visitors alike rave about.

Farm-to-Table Freshness:

Mississippi's agricultural bounty shines through in its farm-to-table dining scene. Explore Jackson's vibrant Farmers Market, where local farmers showcase fresh produce, honey, and artisanal cheeses. At Parlor Market in Jackson, chefs craft seasonal menus that highlight Mississippi-grown ingredients, such as heirloom tomatoes and Gulf seafood. In coastal towns like Bay St. Louis, waterfront restaurants like The Blind Tiger offer seafood straight from the Gulf, paired with locally sourced vegetables and herbs that elevate every dish.

Sweet Tea and Southern Hospitality:

No meal in Mississippi is complete without a glass of sweet tea, a quintessential Southern beverage that's as refreshing as it is steeped in tradition. Whether you're dining at a roadside diner or a fine dining establishment, you'll find sweet tea served with a smile and a side of genuine Southern hospitality that makes every meal memorable.

Chapter 9: Practical Information

Getting There and Around

By Air

Jackson-Medgar Wiley Evers International Airport (JAN) serves as the main gateway for air travelers to Mississippi. Located just a short drive from downtown Jackson, JAN offers connections to major hubs across the United States, making it convenient for both domestic and international visitors. Rental car services are readily available at the airport, providing flexibility for exploring beyond the city limits.

By Road

For those driving into Mississippi, several major highways provide easy access from neighboring states:

Interstate 55 (I-55): Runs north-south through Mississippi, connecting Memphis, Tennessee, to New Orleans, Louisiana, passing through Jackson and other major cities.

Interstate 20 (I-20): East-west route that crosses Mississippi, connecting Dallas, Texas, to Atlanta, Georgia, via Jackson and Vicksburg.

Interstate 10 (I-10): Southern route linking Mississippi's Gulf Coast to Mobile, Alabama, and New Orleans, Louisiana.

US Highway 61: Known as the "Blues Highway," it stretches from New Orleans, Louisiana, to Wyoming, Minnesota, passing through the heart of the Mississippi Delta and offering a scenic route for music enthusiasts and history buffs alike.

Mississippi's highways are well-maintained, with ample signage and rest areas along the way. Exploring the state by car allows travelers to venture off the beaten path, discovering charming small towns, scenic overlooks, and historical landmarks that define Mississippi's unique character.

By Rail

Amtrak's Crescent and City of New Orleans routes serve Mississippi, offering convenient rail travel options for visitors. The Crescent route connects New York City to New Orleans, stopping in cities such as Meridian, Mississippi, while the City of New Orleans route runs from Chicago to New Orleans, stopping in Greenwood and Yazoo City,

Mississippi. Train travel provides a relaxed and scenic alternative, with stations conveniently located in downtown areas for easy access to local attractions.

By River

The Mississippi River, a historic waterway that shapes the state's geography and culture, offers opportunities for river cruises and recreational boating. Ports such as Vicksburg and Natchez welcome riverboat passengers, providing a unique perspective on Mississippi's riverside towns and scenic landscapes.

Getting Around Locally

Once in Mississippi, various transportation options make it easy to explore within cities and regions:

Rental Cars: Available at major airports and urban centers, rental cars provide flexibility for exploring at your own pace.

Public Transportation: Larger cities like Jackson offer bus services and taxi options, while ride-sharing services are also widely available.

Biking and Walking: Many cities and towns in Mississippi are pedestrian-friendly, with bike lanes and trails for eco-conscious travelers looking to explore on two wheels.

Accommodation Guide: Best Places to Stay

Jackson

Fairview Inn - Located in the historic Belhaven neighborhood, the Fairview Inn offers luxury accommodations in a beautifully restored mansion. Enjoy elegant rooms, a fine dining restaurant, and proximity to Jackson's museums and attractions.

The Westin Jackson - Situated in the heart of downtown Jackson, The Westin Jackson combines modern amenities with Southern hospitality. The hotel features spacious rooms, an outdoor pool, and easy access to the city's nightlife and cultural venues.

Coastal Mississippi

Beau Rivage Resort & Casino - A landmark on the Biloxi waterfront, Beau Rivage offers upscale rooms with Gulf views, a casino, multiple dining options, and entertainment venues, making it perfect for both relaxation and excitement.

Harrah's Gulf Coast - Another Biloxi favorite, Harrah's Gulf Coast features comfortable rooms, a variety of dining choices, a spa, and a lively casino atmosphere right on the Gulf of Mexico.

Oxford

The Graduate Oxford - Located near the University of Mississippi campus, The Graduate Oxford captures the essence of Oxford's literary charm with stylish rooms, a rooftop bar, and close proximity to local shops and restaurants.

The Inn at Ole Miss - Situated on the university campus, The Inn at Ole Miss offers convenient accommodations for visiting parents and alumni. Enjoy comfortable rooms, Southern hospitality, and easy access to campus events.

Natchez

Monmouth Historic Inn - Experience Southern elegance at the Monmouth Historic Inn, a beautifully restored antebellum mansion. Nestled on landscaped grounds, the inn features luxurious rooms, gourmet dining, and guided tours of the estate.

Linden Bed and Breakfast - Located in a historic townhouse in downtown Natchez, Linden Bed and Breakfast offers Victorian-style rooms, Southern hospitality, and a delicious homemade breakfast each morning.

Vicksburg

Anchuca Historic Mansion & Inn - Step back in time at Anchuca, a Greek Revival mansion turned inn. Located near Vicksburg's historic district, Anchuca offers charming rooms, Southern cuisine, and guided tours of the mansion.

Duff Green Mansion - This beautifully restored antebellum mansion offers luxury accommodations with period furnishings and modern amenities. Enjoy Southern hospitality, lush gardens, and a glimpse into Vicksburg's rich history.

The Mississippi Delta

The Alluvian Hotel - Located in Greenwood, The Alluvian Hotel blends luxury with Mississippi Delta charm. Enjoy spacious rooms, a spa, fine dining at Giardina's, and guided tours of the Delta's cultural attractions.

Shack Up Inn - For a unique experience, stay at the Shack Up Inn in Clarksdale. This rustic accommodation features converted sharecropper shacks with modern amenities, live music, and a laid-back atmosphere.

Travel Resources and Useful Contacts

Getting There and Around

Airports:

Mississippi is serviced by several airports catering to domestic and regional flights:

Jackson-Medgar Wiley Evers International Airport (JAN): Located in Jackson, it's the busiest airport in the state, offering connections to major cities across the U.S.

Gulfport-Biloxi International Airport (GPT): Situated near Biloxi, this airport serves the Gulf Coast region with flights to destinations like Atlanta, Dallas, and Houston.

Tupelo Regional Airport (TUP): Provides connections to major hubs like Memphis and Nashville, ideal for travelers exploring the northeastern parts of the state.

Car Rentals and Transportation:

Major Car Rental Agencies: Enterprise, Hertz, and Avis have branches at all major airports and in urban centers like Jackson, Gulfport, and Biloxi.

Public Transportation: While limited outside of urban areas, Jackson offers a public bus system. Taxis and rideshare services are available in larger cities.

Accommodation Guide: Best Places to Stay

Hotels and Resorts:

Jackson: The Westin Jackson for luxury, Hilton Garden Inn Downtown for convenience.

Biloxi: Beau Rivage Resort & Casino for entertainment, Margaritaville Resort for a beachfront stay.

Natchez: Monmouth Historic Inn for a historic experience, Dunleith Historic Inn for antebellum charm.

Bed and Breakfasts:

Mississippi Delta: The Alluvian Hotel in Greenwood offers luxury accommodations with Southern charm.

Coastal Mississippi: The Roost Ocean Springs provides a quaint, personalized experience near the beach.

Campgrounds and RV Parks:

Tishomingo State Park: Offers scenic campsites amidst rocky outcrops and hiking trails.

Gulf Islands National Seashore: Perfect for RV travelers with beachfront campsites near Biloxi and Ocean Springs.

Travel Resources

Tourist Information Centers:

Visit Mississippi: Official state tourism website offering comprehensive travel guides, event calendars, and travel tips.

Local Visitor Bureaus: Jackson Convention & Visitors Bureau, Coastal Mississippi, and Visit Oxford provide detailed regional information.

Emergency Contacts:

Emergency Services: Dial 911 for emergencies.

Hospitals: University of Mississippi Medical Center (Jackson), Memorial Hospital (Gulfport), Baptist Memorial Hospital (Oxford).

Useful Contacts

Visitor Hotlines:

Visit Mississippi Hotline: 1-800-927-6378 for travel assistance and information on attractions and events.

Jackson Convention & Visitors Bureau: 601-960-1891 for city-specific information and recommendations.

Weather Information:

National Weather Service: Provides up-to-date forecasts and severe weather alerts for Mississippi.

Road Conditions:

Mississippi Department of Transportation: Offers real-time updates on road closures, construction, and traffic conditions.

Conclusion

As we conclude this journey through the Mississippi Travel Guide 2024, we hope you've found inspiration and practical insights to make your visit to the Magnolia State truly unforgettable. Mississippi, with its deep-rooted history, vibrant culture, and diverse landscapes, offers a tapestry of experiences waiting to be explored.

From the lively streets of Jackson, where history and modernity converge, to the tranquil beaches of Coastal Mississippi and the antebellum charm of Natchez, each region of Mississippi tells a unique story. Whether you're drawn to the soulful rhythms of the Delta blues, the literary legacy of Oxford, or the scenic beauty of the Natchez Trace Parkway, there's something here for every traveler.

Throughout this guide, we've provided detailed recommendations on where to go, what to see, and where to stay, ensuring you can tailor your journey to suit your interests and preferences. Whether you're a food enthusiast eager to sample Southern delicacies, an outdoor adventurer seeking hiking trails and scenic drives, or a history buff delving into Civil War sites and antebellum architecture, Mississippi offers abundant opportunities for discovery.

Remember to immerse yourself in local festivals and events, indulge in the flavors of Mississippi's cuisine, and take time to connect with the warm hospitality of its people. Use the practical information provided on transportation, accommodations, and useful contacts to navigate your way seamlessly through the state.

As you depart, we invite you to carry with you the memories of Mississippi's rich cultural heritage and natural beauty. Whether this is your first visit or a return to familiar places, let the spirit of the Magnolia State captivate you once more. Thank you for choosing our guide to accompany you on this journey. May your adventures in Mississippi be filled with joy, discovery, and moments that linger in your heart long after you've returned home.

Safe travels, and until we meet again in the heart of the South.

Printed in Great Britain
by Amazon